FRE
MEALS FROM THE HOB

FRESH & FAST: MEALS FROM THE HOB

Annette Yates and Norma Miller

RIGHT WAY

Typeset in 9½ pt Swiss 721 by Letterpart Ltd., Reigate, Surrey.

Printed and bound in Great Britain by Cox & Wyman Ltd., Reading, Berkshire.

The *Right Way* series is published by Elliot Right Way Books, Brighton Road, Lower Kingswood, Tadworth, Surrey, KT20 6TD, U.K. For information about our company and the other books we publish, visit our website at www.right-way.co.uk

CONTENTS

Front cover recipe: Chilli Chicken, page 76.

Photograph by Michael Kay, Solar Studios, Croydon.

Food styling by Taste Talk.

INTRODUCTION

Like most people today we want to eat real food, something we have prepared ourselves. We want freshly cooked meals in place of ready meals. While our lives seem to become more hectic, as food writers and running a creative food business, with husbands who are equally busy, we want food on the table fast. Something that makes more of food than a quick take-away.

To us, fast food means making quick dishes, using a mixture of fresh and store cupboard ingredients – all readily obtainable from food stores.

This book helps you to do just that, without spending hours slaving in the kitchen. The pages are bursting with foolproof recipes that are impressive and delicious, quick and easy to make, and all tried and tested by us. And we've given plenty of serving suggestions and hints and tips to make life even easier.

Whether you are cooking for yourself, your family or for friends, there's a recipe for every occasion. And they can all be rustled up in next to no time.

Don't forget, even when time is tight food can be fast!

RECIPE GUIDELINES

For convenience, the ingredients are listed in the order in which they are used. Though they are given in imperial measurements as well as metric, you will find the metric easier to use.

All spoon measures are level unless otherwise stated.

Most of the recipes can produce extra servings, simply by doubling the quantity of ingredients; for some, you may need to use an extra pan.

The recipes include basic store cupboard ingredients, including the occasional stock cube and, our favourite, vegetable bouillon powder. Because it's granular, you can spoon out as little as you like. Our store cupboard always contains canned tomatoes, a selection of canned beans, and small jars of pastes that are so quick and convenient – garlic, curry and chilli.

One or two recipes may contain raw or partly cooked eggs – please remember that it is advisable to avoid eating these if you are pregnant, elderly, very young or sick.

A few recipes contain fresh chillies. Do take care when preparing them and remember to wash your hands thoroughly afterwards. Better still, wear rubber gloves while handling them.

Salt is kept to a minimum. Instead, we prefer to source good quality ingredients that have bags of flavour. By cooking quickly on the hob maximum flavours and colours are retained. Often, just a handful of freshly chopped herbs is all you need to boost flavour.

The equipment is kept simple. For example, nothing requires the use of a food processor. Instead we use a stick blender for whizzing soups into chunky or smooth blends (if you don't have one, then of course a food processor is fine). With pans, it's best to think big – use a wide, shallow pan, a wok or, for cooking pasta, a deep pan with plenty of room. Non-stick surfaces save on the washing up too.

1

START THE DAY

Breakfast is often a hurried meal, unless you are lucky enough to be able to take it leisurely, or can turn it into brunch. So by-passing the usual familiar fare – muesli, fresh fruit, bacon and eggs – here are some new twists on traditional themes. Some of these recipes can be polished off in no time at all, before dashing out of the house. Try a healthy smoothie or a bowl of warm fruit, or liven up your eggs with tomatoes, couscous and peppers. Mostly the recipes use just one pan.

....healthy and good lookin'

s m o o t h i e

Mushroom and Bacon Egg-Dipped Sandwich

Egg-dipped bread is a childhood favourite. Here, the tasty mushroom and bacon filling makes a substantial start to the day. You could use turkey rashers in place of bacon or vary the mushrooms – try oyster, chestnut or shiitake.

Serves 2

2 lean back bacon rashers
6 button mushrooms
2 tomatoes
3 medium eggs
2 tbsp milk
1 tsp freshly chopped parsley
Freshly milled black pepper
4 brown or white bread slices
1 tbsp vegetable oil
Few drops of hot pepper sauce (optional)

1. With scissors, cut the rind from the bacon rashers then cut the bacon into small pieces. Finely chop the mushrooms and tomatoes.

2. Break the eggs into a wide, shallow dish and beat in the milk, chopped parsley and black pepper.

3. Arrange the bread slices in a single layer in a shallow dish and pour the egg mixture over. With a fish slice, carefully turn the slices over until the egg mixture has been absorbed.

4. Heat a small pan and add a little of the oil. Tip in the chopped bacon, mushrooms and tomatoes. Cook quickly for about 5 minutes, stirring occasionally, until cooked through. If wished, add a few drops of hot pepper sauce, to taste.

5. Spoon the mushroom mixture onto two slices of the bread. Spread the filling almost to the edges and cover each with a remaining slice of bread, pressing well down, to give two sandwiches.

6. Heat a large non-stick frying pan and add a little of the oil. Cook the sandwiches on both sides until crisp and golden, adding more oil if necessary.

7. Cut the sandwiches in half diagonally and serve immediately.

Eggs Mediterranean Style

One of our favourite brunch dishes – quick, easy and full of flavour. Serve it with warm, crusty bread.

Serves 2 or 4 depending on appetites

2 tbsp couscous
1 red pepper
3 spring onions
400g can chopped tomatoes
1 tbsp freshly chopped parsley
Freshly milled salt and black pepper
4 medium eggs

1. Put the couscous into a small bowl and cover with boiling water.

2. Cut the pepper in half, remove and discard the stalk and seeds, and slice thinly. Trim and thinly slice the spring onions.

3. Tip the tomatoes into a wide, shallow pan and bring just to the boil. Stir in the sliced pepper and spring onions and cook gently for 3–4 minutes.

4. Meanwhile drain the couscous in a fine sieve, pressing to remove as much water as possible.

5. Stir the couscous and chopped parsley into the tomato mixture and season to taste.

6. Make four wells in the mixture and crack an egg into each space.

7. Cook gently until the eggs are set and serve immediately.

Scrambled Eggs with Smoked Salmon

A little smoked salmon goes a long way by allowing it to infuse the milk with its flavour. Why not add some chives, parsley or dill to the beaten eggs? Serve it hot, piled onto slices of freshly toasted granary bread.

Serves 2

100g/3½ oz smoked salmon slices
4 tbsp milk
4 large or 5 medium eggs
Freshly milled pepper

1. Cut the salmon into short strips, put them into a small bowl and stir in the milk. Leave to stand for 10–15 minutes if time allows.

2. Break the eggs into a bowl, season with pepper and beat lightly with a fork. Pour them into a non-stick pan.

3. Cook the eggs over a medium heat, stirring continuously, until the eggs begin to thicken but there is still plenty of liquid.

4. Add the salmon and milk and continue cooking, stirring gently, until the eggs are almost set. At this stage remove the pan from the heat – the eggs will finish cooking in the heat of the pan.

5. Serve immediately.

Savoury Salmon Rice

This recipe is based on the well-known dish called kedgeree. It's great for special occasions, high days and holidays, breakfast, brunch or lunch. Try making it with basmati rice with smoked trout in place of salmon.

Serves 2

2 medium eggs
125g/4½ oz long grain rice
75g/2¾ oz smoked salmon
25g/1 oz butter
Freshly milled pepper
2 tbsp freshly chopped parsley
Lemon wedges, to serve

1. Put the eggs in a small pan, cover with water, bring to the boil and cook gently for 10 minutes.

2. Cook the rice following the packet instructions.

3. Meanwhile, cut the salmon into short strips.

4. Drain the eggs, cover with cold water and leave to cool slightly. Peel off the shells and cut into quarters.

5. Drain the rice and stir in the butter until melted. Season with pepper and gently fold in the salmon, eggs and parsley.

6. Serve with lemon wedges for squeezing over.

Crusted Herrings with Vine Tomatoes and Focaccia

Your fishmonger will be happy to clean the fish – ask for the heads to be removed if you prefer. Try other oily fish too, such as sardines.

Serves 2

4 small to medium herrings
2 small red apples
2 tbsp cornmeal or polenta
Pinch of mustard powder
Freshly milled salt and pepper
2 tbsp oil
2 sprigs of cherry tomatoes, 5–6 on each vine
4 small slices of herb focaccia bread
Lemon wedges, to serve

1. Wash the herrings under cold, running water. Quarter the apples, remove and discard the core, and cut each apple into eight wedges.

2. On a large plate, mix together the cornmeal or polenta and mustard powder. Season with salt and pepper. Dip the fish in the seasoned cornmeal, turning until coated.

3. Heat 1 tbsp oil in a non-stick frying pan, add the herrings and cook quickly for 1–2 minutes on each side or until cooked through.

4. Meanwhile, heat the remaining oil in another shallow pan. Add the apple wedges and the tomatoes (still on their stalks) and cook for 2–3 minutes, turning once until soft and golden brown.

5. Toast the bread and top with the herrings. Add the hot apple and tomatoes.

6. Serve with lemon wedges for squeezing over.

Hot Oat and Blueberry Smoothie

Breakfast in a mug! If you like smoothies, you will love this. The oats are just softened rather than cooked to give a lovely texture. Use your favourite soft fruits – fresh or frozen.

Serves 1–2

2 ready-to-eat dried apricots
300ml/½ pint milk
2 tbsp quick porridge oats
150ml/¼ pint unsweetened apple juice
A small handful of blueberries
Clear honey (optional)
A few sunflower seeds

1. Roughly chop the apricots.

2. Pour the milk into a small pan and bring just to the boil. Reduce the heat and stir in the porridge oats and chopped apricots. Cook gently for 1–2 minutes, stirring once or twice.

3. Remove the pan from the heat and stir in the apple juice and blueberries. Sweeten to taste with a little honey.

4. Serve just as it is or, for a smoother version, whizz with a stick blender.

5. Pour into large mugs or heatproof glasses and scatter a few sunflower seeds over the top.

Prunes in Blackcurrant and Lemon

We use the herbal infusions for a light flavour. If you enjoy the taste of tea, use blackcurrant-flavoured tea bags instead. It's good hot or cold – eat some straight away and keep the rest in the fridge for the next few days. And it makes a good dessert too, served with a dollop of thick yogurt or a scoop of vanilla ice cream and maybe sprinkled with a few chopped pistachios or hazelnuts.

Serves 4

½ lemon
250g/9 oz ready-to-eat dried prunes
2 tbsp soft brown sugar
3 blackcurrant infusion bags

1. With a potato peeler, thinly peel the lemon rind, making sure no white pith is attached, and cut into very thin strips. Squeeze the juice from the lemon.

2. Put the lemon rind and juice into a medium saucepan and add the prunes, sugar, infusion bags and about 300ml/½ pint water.

3. Bring just to the boil, cover and cook gently for 5 minutes.

4. Remove from the heat and leave to stand for about 10 minutes, or longer if time allows.

5. Discard the infusion bags before serving.

American-Style Pancakes

These light, fluffy pancakes are really impressive, yet quick to make. You could sprinkle them with a few fresh berries – blueberries, raspberries – before the top surface has had a chance to set. Then simply flip over to cook the second side. Serve with crisp-fried bacon drizzled with maple syrup. Or think about serving them for dessert, topped with ricotta, thick yogurt or whipped cream, fruit and honey.

Makes 8 pancakes measuring about 10cm/4 inch across

100g/3½ oz plain flour
2 tsp baking powder
Pinch of salt
1 large egg
125ml/4 fl oz milk
Oil

1. Sift the flour, baking powder and salt into a bowl or jug. Make a well in the centre and break in the egg. With a whisk, gently stir the flour into the egg, gradually adding the milk, to make a smooth thick batter. If time allows, cover and leave to stand for about 15 minutes.

2. Brush a griddle or non-stick frying pan lightly with oil and put over a medium heat. When the pan is hot, pour in a spoonful or two of batter. Cook gently for about 2 minutes, or until the underside is golden brown and the bubbles that rise to the surface begin to pop. Carefully flip the pancake over and cook the second side for about 1 minute. Lift out and keep warm.

3. Cook the remaining batter, making about 8 pancakes in total, and serve warm.

2

SNAPPY SNACKS

Feeling peckish? A snappy snack can satisfy the most sudden onrush of appetite. A bought-in sandwich might well suffice, but a toasted sandwich, butter-side out, with a favourite filling and toasted in a hot pan will really hit the spot.

These quick bites and snacks are suitable for any time of the day, whenever you feel like treating yourself or you are in need of a pick-me-up. The recipes can all be rustled up in a few minutes and, if you serve them with a salad and bread, they can easily turn into light meals.

v e g e t a b l e   t o a s t s

Bruschetta with Tuna Mayonnaise

Choose Italian-style bread such as ciabatta or focaccia; seeded wholegrain bread is good too. Cooking the bread in a griddle pan gives the best 'charred' flavour. Use tuna in oil or brine, whichever you prefer.

Serves 2

200g can tuna
A few cherry tomatoes
1 tbsp capers
2 anchovy fillets (optional)
1 garlic clove
1 tbsp mayonnaise
1 tbsp thick natural yogurt
1 tbsp fresh lemon juice
Freshly milled black pepper
About 1 tbsp freshly chopped parsley, plus extra for garnish
Thick bread slices
1–2 tbsp olive oil

1. Drain the tuna. Halve the tomatoes. Drain, wash, dry and roughly chop the capers and the anchovies (if using). Cut the garlic clove in half.

2. Flake the tuna into a bowl and stir in the mayonnaise, yogurt, lemon juice, black pepper and the parsley. Stir until well mixed.

3. Toast bread slices on a preheated griddle pan or frying pan, under a hot grill or in a toaster.

4. Meanwhile, heat a separate small pan and add the oil. Add the tomatoes, capers and anchovies and stir over a medium heat until the tomatoes soften slightly and every-thing is heated through.

5. Rub one side of each hot toast with the cut side of garlic and top with a generous dollop of the tuna mixture. Spoon the tomato mixture (with all its juices) over and finish with a sprinkling of parsley. Don't wait, eat!

Smoked Trout and Walnuts on Ciabatta

Flakes of smoked trout and broken walnuts are folded into a creamy cheese sauce, spooned onto toasted ciabatta and grilled until bubbling. We like to use a smooth tomato relish but you could use your favourite relish, chutney or even brown sauce.

Serves 4

2 cooked smoked trout fillets, about 225g/8 oz total weight
3 gherkins
5 walnut halves
225g/8 oz mature hard cheese, such as Cheddar or Red Leicester
300ml/½ pint milk
2 tbsp beer, dry white wine or milk
25g/1 oz butter
25g/1 oz plain flour
1 tsp made mustard
2 tbsp tomato relish
Freshly milled pepper
8 slices of herb ciabatta bread

1. Peel the skin from the trout and flake the fish, removing any bones. Slice the gherkins and break the nuts into small pieces. Grate the cheese, reserving a little for sprinkling over.

2. Pour the milk into a medium pan, add the beer or white wine (or extra milk) and butter, and tip in the flour. Bring to the boil, beating with a whisk (a coil type is best), for 3–5 minutes or until thickened and smooth.

3. Add the cheese and mustard. Stirring continuously, cook gently until the cheese has melted.

4. Remove the pan from the heat and gently fold in the flaked trout, gherkins, walnuts and relish. Season if necessary.

5. Meanwhile, heat the grill and toast the ciabatta slices on one side. Remove from the heat, turn the bread and spoon the cheese and fish mixture over. Sprinkle over the reserved cheese and grill until bubbling and piping hot.

Mushroom and Prawn Scramble on Bagels

Scrambled egg with a twist! Make sure you buy cooked prawns (in other words, they are pink) though you can add them fresh or frozen.

Serves 2

175g/6 oz mixed mushrooms, such as shiitake, button, chestnut, oyster
2 sprigs of fresh oregano
2 tomatoes
4 medium eggs
2 tbsp single cream or milk
Freshly milled black pepper
2 bagels
2 tsp olive oil
1 tbsp tomato purée
25g/1 oz butter
100g/3½ oz cooked shelled prawns
1 tsp lemon juice
Freshly chopped parsley

1. Clean and trim the mushrooms and slice thinly. Strip the leaves from the oregano sprigs. If time allows, skin the tomatoes by pricking them with a fork, putting them into a small bowl or cup and covering with boiling water. After a minute or two, pour off the water and carefully remove the skin. Chop the tomatoes roughly.

2. Break the eggs into a small bowl and mix together with the cream or milk and oregano leaves. Season with pepper.

3. Slice each bagel into three rings. Brush each cut surface with a little oil and then tomato purée.

4. Heat a non-stick frying pan and 'toast' the bagel slices until piping hot.

5. Meanwhile melt the butter in a small pan, add the mushrooms and cook quickly for a minute or two until golden. Add the prawns and lemon juice and cook until heated through. Pour in the egg mixture and cook gently, stirring the set egg away from the sides, until the mixture is only just scrambled.

6. Spoon onto the hot bagel slices and serve immediately sprinkled with parsley.

Hot Bacon Pitta Toasts

This includes a version of the Middle Eastern spread called hummus. This one is made with beans instead of the more usual chickpeas. We just pile it all onto a plate for eating with a knife and fork but you could just as well split the warm pittas and fill them with the bacon and the bean spread. When doubling or tripling quantities, it may be more convenient to use a stick blender or processor to break up the beans.

Serves 2

200g can beans, such as cannellini or flageolet
1 small garlic clove
1 tbsp tahini (sesame paste) or peanut butter
2 tbsp thick natural yogurt
1 tbsp fresh lemon juice
¼ tsp ground cumin
Freshly milled salt and black pepper
1 tsp olive oil
4 bacon rashers
2 pitta bread

1. Drain the beans, reserving the liquid. Finely chop or crush the garlic.

2. Put the beans into a shallow bowl and add the garlic, tahini or peanut butter, yogurt, lemon juice, cumin and seasoning. With a fork, mash until well mixed, adding a little of the reserved bean liquid if necessary until the mixture is still thick and chunky.

3. Heat a large non-stick frying pan, add the oil and bacon and cook over a medium heat until slightly crisp and golden brown on both sides. Either move the bacon right to the edge of the pan or lift it out and keep warm.

4. Add the pitta breads to the pan and, using a spatula to hold them flat, heat through quickly on both sides (it's nice if they brown and crisp a bit too).

5. Lift out onto warmed serving plates and top with the bean mixture and the crispy bacon.

Goats' Cheese with Tapenade on Crumpets

Tapenade is a black olive spread flavoured with anchovy fillets and capers. Here is our home-made version but you could of course buy your favourite brand instead. It may be more convenient to use a stick blender or processor to break up the beans, particularly when making a larger quantity.

Serves 4

6–8 cherry tomatoes
1 garlic clove
140g/5 oz goats' cheese log
50g/1¾ oz stoned black olives
2 anchovy fillets
50g/1¾ oz capers
1 tbsp olive oil
1 tsp lemon juice
Freshly milled black pepper
4 crumpets
Small salad leaves, to serve

1. Halve the cherry tomatoes. Crush the garlic clove. Slice the cheese into four.

2. Finely chop the olives, anchovy fillets and capers and spoon into a small bowl. Add the crushed garlic and slowly stir in the oil and lemon juice. Season with black pepper.

3. Toast the crumpets.

4. Heat a non-stick frying pan and when very hot add the slices of goats' cheese, cut side down, with the halved tomatoes. Cook for a few seconds until the cheese softens. Turn the cheese and the tomatoes over and cook a further few seconds.

5. Spread each crumpet with some tapenade and top with the hot cheese and tomatoes. Serve immediately with salad leaves.

Sizzled Vegetable Toasts

We like to spread the toast with quark, a mild curd cheese that has a slightly sour flavour. Cream cheese works well too, or try using the bean mixture on page 26 instead. If you are preparing one or two portions, it's easy to use just the one pan. For larger amounts, you will probably need one pan for the vegetables and another for the toast (a griddle pan is good).

Serves 1

1 small courgette
1 small red pepper
4 cherry tomatoes
1 spring onion
2 tsp olive oil
1 small garlic clove
Wine or sherry vinegar
Thick slice of bread
2 generous tbsp curd cheese, such as quark, or cream cheese
Freshly milled black pepper

1. Cut the courgette lengthways into thin slices. Halve the pepper, remove and discard the seeds and stalk, and slice thinly. Halve the tomatoes and thinly slice the spring onion.

2. Heat a shallow non-stick frying pan, add the oil, courgette and red pepper. Cook over a medium heat, stirring occasionally, until softened and lightly browned.

3. Stir in the garlic, tomatoes and spring onion and cook for 1–2 minutes. Sprinkle over a little wine/sherry vinegar (to taste) then lift out and keep warm.

4. Put the bread into the hot pan, increase the heat and toast it until crisp and golden on both sides. Lift out.

5. Spread a generous amount of cheese over the hot toast and season with a little black pepper.

6. Spoon the hot vegetables over the top and eat!

Spice-Fried Potatoes

Don't be put off using canned new potatoes – they are brilliant in this spicy dish. Serve it just as it is, with salad or (our favourite) with a spoonful or two of natural yogurt flavoured with chopped fresh mint or coriander. It also makes a good side dish with burgers, sausages, chops, chicken or fish. You could make it more substantial too, by adding extra ingredients at the end of step 2, such as thinly sliced red onion, slivers of bacon or thin strips of chicken.

Serves 1–2

550g can baby potatoes
1 tbsp oil
½ tsp mustard seeds
½ tsp fennel seeds
1 tsp curry powder
Handful of chopped fresh coriander
Lemon wedges to serve

1. Drain the potatoes well and pat dry with kitchen paper.

2. Heat the oil in a non-stick pan and stir in the mustard seeds. As soon as they begin to pop, add the fennel seeds and curry powder, stirring well.

3. Add the potatoes and shake the pan, coating them well with the spice mixture.

4. Cook over a medium heat for 5–10 minutes, shaking the pan or stirring occasionally, until the potatoes are golden brown and heated through.

5. Throw in the coriander and serve with lemon wedges for squeezing over.

Mexican Refried Beans

The Mexican name for this spicy dish is Frijoles Refritos and literally means twice-cooked beans. We've made this with other beans and it is very successful. If you like extra heat use jalapeño chillies. Make sure you use a wide, shallow pan – the mixture will cook more efficiently.

Serves 4–6

1 onion
2 garlic cloves
400g can red kidney beans or pinto beans
2 red chillies (see page 8)
2 tomatoes
2 tbsp olive oil
Freshly milled black pepper
Tortilla chips, to serve
Soured cream, to serve

1. Finely chop the onion and crush the garlic. Drain the beans, reserving the liquid. Slice the chillies very finely (remove the seeds if you want a milder flavour).

2. To skin the tomatoes, prick them with a fork, put them into a small bowl or cup, cover with boiling water and, after a minute or two, pour off the water and carefully remove the skin. Roughly chop the tomatoes.

3. Put the beans into a shallow bowl and add the onion, garlic, chillies and tomatoes. With a fork, mash until well mixed but not too smooth, adding a little of the reserved bean liquid if necessary.

4. Heat a wide non-stick pan and add the oil. Spoon in the crushed bean mixture and, stirring frequently, cook until it is piping hot. Add some of the reserved liquid if the mixture is too stiff – it should be creamy and dry. Season if necessary.

5. Serve piping hot with tortilla chips to dunk into the bean mixture and soured cream to blob on top.

3

INSTANT SOUPS

Soups are so many good things: savoury, stimulating, reassuring, revitalising. Even when quick to prepare, they can still be wholesome and really rewarding. None of these soups should take longer than about thirty minutes to cook, and the fastest will be ready in just eight minutes.

You can try our own version of soup-in-a-cup, flavoured with mushroom and lemon. You will also find light, refreshing soups here, and some much more substantial ones with pasta, sausage or lentils.

You can ring the changes by adapting these recipes for different uses too. As a starter, add croûtons to a small bowl of soup or serve it with a selection of breads. Alternatively, ladle a generous serving into a large bowl, accompany with crusty bread and make a meal of it.

This is the section where a stick blender comes into its own for whizzing soups (still in the pan) into chunky or smooth blends, though you could of course use a food processor instead.

Lemon Mushroom Soup in a Mug

A really speedy soup which is also very light and refreshing. For a change, make it with a mixture of mushrooms such as chestnut, oyster and chanterelle. Norma really loves this soup made with the herb lemon myrtle in place of the lemon juice.

Serves 1

5 button mushrooms
1 spring onion
1 tsp vegetable oil
300ml/½ pint vegetable stock
1 tbsp lemon juice
Freshly milled salt and pepper

1. Clean and trim the mushrooms, then slice thinly. Thinly slice the spring onion.

2. Heat the oil in a small pan, add the sliced spring onion and mushrooms and cook on a medium heat for 2–3 minutes until lightly browned.

3. Pour in the stock and lemon juice and bring to the boil. Reduce the heat and cook gently for 5 minutes. Season if necessary.

4. Pour into a large mug or bowl and enjoy!

Tomato and Orange Pasta Soup

The flavour of orange adds freshness to this substantial soup. Soup pasta is often neglected – try using tiny shapes such as stars, shells, spirals or alphabet. Delicious served with hot crusty bread.

Serves 4

2 shallots
1 tsp olive oil
400g can chopped tomatoes
300ml/½ pint vegetable stock
1 tsp Worcestershire sauce
300ml/½ pint unsweetened orange juice
1 tbsp lemon juice
50g/1¾ oz small soup pasta
A small handful of fresh basil leaves
Freshly milled salt and pepper
Low fat yogurt

1. Finely chop the shallots.

2. Heat the oil in a medium pan and add the chopped shallots. Cook over a gentle heat for about 5 minutes until softened and lightly browned.

3. Stir in the tomatoes, stock, Worcestershire sauce, orange and lemon juice and then bring to the boil.

4. Add the soup pasta, bring back to the boil, stirring once or twice, and cook for the time indicated on the packet.

5. Stir in the basil leaves, season if necessary and ladle into bowls. Swirl a spoonful of yogurt into each bowl, then serve immediately with extra yogurt.

Noodle, Leaf and Mushroom Soup

A light soup with an oriental flavour. For a milder result, omit the chilli seeds. For speed, you could use straight-to-wok noodles. Add a little crunch by stirring in a handful of fresh bean sprouts just before serving.

Serves 4–6

75g/2¾ oz mushrooms, such as shiitake or chestnut
1 small head of Chinese leaves
1 garlic clove
Small piece of fresh root ginger
1 red chilli (see page 8)
½ lime
1 tbsp light soy sauce
1 beef or chicken stock cube
85g/3 oz noodles
Handful of coriander leaves

1. Clean and trim the mushrooms and slice thinly. Thinly slice the Chinese leaves. Finely chop the garlic, ginger and chilli. Squeeze the juice from the lime.

2. Pour 1 litre/1¾ pints water into a saucepan and add the soy sauce, stock cube, garlic, ginger, chilli and lime. Bring just to the boil, reduce the heat and cook gently for 5 minutes.

3. Stir in the noodles, Chinese leaves and mushrooms. Cook gently for 3–5 minutes or until the noodles are cooked (follow the cooking time on the packet).

4. Stir in the coriander and serve immediately.

Parsnip and Mustard Soup

We've used wholegrain mustard here – for variety's sake, try Dijon, English or German. Serve it with crunchy croûtons or hot, thick slices of toast.

Serves 4–6

1 medium onion
1 garlic clove
500g/1 lb 2 oz parsnips
1 large potato
1 tbsp oil
1 litre/1¾ pints vegetable stock
2 tbsp wholegrain mustard
Freshly milled salt and pepper

1. Finely chop the onion and the garlic. Peel and thinly slice the parsnips and potato.

2. Heat the oil in a large saucepan and add the onion and garlic. Cook gently for about 5 minutes, stirring occasionally, until beginning to soften but not brown.

3. Add the parsnips, potato and stock and bring to the boil. Reduce the heat, cover and cook gently for 15–20 minutes or until the vegetables are very soft.

4. Using a stick blender, whizz until fairly smooth, adding a little extra water if necessary.

5. Stir in the mustard and season lightly with salt and pepper.

6. Reheat and serve.

Green Lentil Soup with Red Onion and Spinach

Green lentils need no soaking before cooking. For a smooth soup use a stick blender in step 4, before adding the spinach leaves, and whizz until smooth. Serve it with warm pitta bread.

Serves 3–4

1 large red onion
2 carrots
1 garlic clove
2 handfuls of young spinach leaves
1 tbsp olive oil
225g/8 oz large green lentils
1 litre/1¾ pints vegetable stock
1 bay leaf
Freshly milled black pepper

1. Finely chop the red onion and the carrots and crush the garlic clove. Thoroughly wash the spinach leaves and shake off any excess water.

2. Heat the oil in a large pan and stir in the chopped onion and carrots. Cook the vegetables on a medium heat for 5 minutes, stirring once or twice. Add the garlic and cook for 1 minute.

3. Add the green lentils, vegetable stock and bay leaf. Bring just to the boil, reduce the heat and cook for 10 minutes (or the time indicated on the packet).

4. Remove the bay leaf, stir the spinach leaves into the pan and cook for a further 2–3 minutes until they have just wilted.

5. Season if necessary and serve.

Smoked Haddock Chowder

Chowder is a thick, chunky soup. This one is made with smoked haddock (we prefer the undyed sort) and frozen or drained canned sweetcorn. A little thick cream stirred in just before serving adds a touch of luxury. Serve with crusty bread.

Serves 4–6

1 medium onion
4 celery sticks
225g/8 oz new potatoes
About 250g/9 oz skinless smoked haddock
1 tbsp oil
600ml/1 pint vegetable stock
600ml/1 pint milk
175g/6 oz sweetcorn kernels
Freshly milled pepper
Freshly chopped parsley

1. Finely chop the onion and celery. Cut the potatoes into very small cubes. Remove any visible bones from the haddock and cut into bite-size pieces.

2. Heat the oil in a large saucepan and add the onion, celery and potatoes. Cook over a medium heat for 5–10 minutes, stirring occasionally, until the vegetables begin to soften but not brown.

3. Add the stock and bring just to the boil. Reduce the heat, cover and cook gently for about 10 minutes until the potatoes are soft.

4. Stir in the haddock, then add the milk and sweetcorn. Season with pepper.

5. Heat through gently until the haddock begins to flake and is cooked through.

6. Serve topped with a sprinkling of parsley.

Curried Chicken Soup with Mango Chutney

A hot, hot soup, well not fiery hot! Choose a mild or hot curry powder; add a little chilli for extra oomph. It's lovely topped with a spoonful of yogurt or single cream and sprinkled with a few toasted flaked almonds. If you can't buy minced chicken, simply use finely chopped chicken breast.

Serves 4

1 large onion
2 streaky bacon rashers
2 tsp oil
175g/6 oz minced chicken
2 tsp mild curry powder
850ml/1½ pints chicken stock
1 tbsp smooth mango chutney
1 tbsp lemon juice
Freshly milled salt and pepper
Cooked poppadoms, to serve

1. Finely chop the onion. With scissors, cut the rind from the bacon rashers then cut the bacon into small pieces.

2. Heat the oil in a large pan, add the chopped onion and bacon and cook on a medium heat for 5 minutes, stirring occasionally.

3. Add the chicken and cook for about 10 minutes, stirring and breaking up the chicken with a metal spoon.

4. Stir in the curry powder, pour the stock over and bring just to the boil. Reduce the heat and cook gently for about 5 minutes until the chicken is cooked through.

5. Stir in the mango chutney and lemon juice, then season if necessary.

6. Serve with poppadoms.

Stir-Fry Beef and Vegetable Soup

This stir-fry-in-a-bowl makes a substantial soup! This version includes thread noodles, though rice, buckwheat or soba noodles would make excellent alternatives.

Serves 4–6

175g/6 oz rump steak
3 tbsp soy sauce
2 garlic cloves
Small piece of fresh ginger
1 small head of Chinese leaves
100g/3½ oz mushrooms, such as chestnut or oyster
50g/1¾ oz mange-touts
1 small yellow or red pepper
4 spring onions
1 tbsp oil
1.2 litres/2 pints beef or vegetable stock, or a mixture
85g/3 oz thread noodles
Freshly milled salt and black pepper
2 tbsp chopped fresh coriander or parsley

1. Cut the steak into thin strips, toss with the soy sauce and leave to stand while you prepare the other ingredients. Finely chop the garlic and ginger. Thinly slice the Chinese leaves, mushrooms and mange-touts. Halve the pepper, remove and discard the seeds and stalk, and cut into small pieces. Thinly slice the spring onions.

2. Heat the oil in a large pan or wok, add the beef and cook over a high heat, stirring, until golden brown.

3. Add the garlic and ginger and cook, stirring, for 1 minute. Add the mushrooms, pepper and mange-touts. Cook for 1–2 minutes, stirring.

4. Add the stock and break the noodles into the pan.

5. Add the Chinese leaves and spring onions and bring just to the boil. Reduce the heat and cook gently for 3–5 minutes until the noodles are soft.

6. Season to taste and stir in the coriander or parsley.

Spicy Sausage, Leek and Potato Soup

Choose a spicy sausage such as Spanish chorizo or German bratwurst. Peppered salami works well too. There is no need to peel new potatoes.

Serves 4–6

100g/3½ oz spicy sausage, preferably in one piece
2 medium leeks
About 400g/14 oz potatoes
1 tbsp oil
850ml/1½ pints chicken or vegetable stock
Freshly milled salt and black pepper
150ml/¼ pint milk
Handful of chopped parsley

1. Cut the sausage into small cubes. Thinly slice the leeks. Peel and thinly slice the potatoes.

2. Heat the oil in a large saucepan, add the sausage and cook quickly, stirring frequently, until golden brown. With a draining spoon, lift out and put to one side.

3. To the same pan, add the leeks and potatoes. Cook over a medium heat for 5–10 minutes, stirring occasionally, until beginning to soften and turn golden brown. Add the stock and season with pepper only at this stage. Bring to the boil, reduce the heat and cook gently for 15–20 minutes or until the vegetables are very soft.

4. Add the milk. With a stick blender, whizz until fairly smooth, adding a little extra water if the mixture is too thick.

5. Stir in the sausage and, if necessary, season with a little salt and pepper.

6. Reheat gently until piping hot, stir in the parsley and serve.

4

WARM SALADS

For some hot savoury additions to nestle into those crisp, cool salad leaves, remember your hob is at hand. For fast and impressive bistro-style results, pan-fry slices of chicken or duck, fish steaks or cheese, and transfer them quickly to your pre-arranged and dressed salad. Then, if served straight away, the leaves will just start to wilt from the contact and the hot pan juices will slip instantly and deliciously into the salad dressing.

Some of these hot salads can go into the refrigerator and be served cold and still appetising on the following day.

h o t   d u c k

Halloumi and Asparagus with Mustard Seed Dressing

Halloumi is a cheese made from goats' milk, usually from Cyprus, that holds its shape well during cooking and needs no extra fat in the pan.

Serves 4 as a starter or 2 as a main course

8 asparagus spears
1 cucumber
175g/6 oz halloumi cheese
3 tbsp olive oil
4 tsp balsamic vinegar
1 tsp clear honey
Freshly milled salt and pepper
1 tsp white mustard seeds
Small spinach leaves
85g/3 oz mixed black and green pitted olives
1 tbsp freshly grated Parmesan cheese

1. Trim the 'woody' part from the base of the asparagus spears. Cut the cucumber in half lengthways and with a small spoon scrape out and discard the seeds. Slice the cucumber very thinly. Cut the halloumi into strips.

2. Cook the asparagus spears in boiling water for a few minutes until just tender. Drain and cool in cold water (this will stop the asparagus from cooking further and becoming too soft). Drain on kitchen paper and cut each spear into two or three pieces.

3. Pour the olive oil into a shallow bowl and mix in the balsamic vinegar, honey and seasoning.

4. Heat a non-stick frying pan, when hot add the mustard seeds and heat for a few seconds until they begin to pop. Tip them onto a plate and put to one side. Return the pan to the heat and when hot arrange the halloumi slices in a single layer. Cook quickly on both sides until lightly browned.

5. Scatter the spinach leaves in a large bowl, add the sliced cucumber, asparagus spears, olives, hot halloumi and mustard seeds and quickly mix together. Drizzle the dressing over, sprinkle with the Parmesan cheese and eat straight away.

Rice Salad with Feta and Olives

The long grain rice in this salad could be replaced with basmati, brown or red Camargue. It's a salad that is best served at room temperature.

Serves 2

125g/4½ oz long grain rice
4 spring onions
½ small lemon
2 tbsp olive oil
1 generous tsp clear honey
1 generous tsp wholegrain mustard
Freshly milled salt and black pepper
125g/4½ oz feta cheese
Small handful of pitted olives – green, black or a mixture
Handful of fresh mint or parsley

1. Cook the rice following the packet instructions and drain.

2. Meanwhile, thinly slice the spring onions. Finely grate the rind of the lemon and squeeze out its juice. Whisk together the oil, lemon rind and juice, honey and mustard.

3. Tip the drained rice into a serving bowl, add the oil mixture and stir gently together. Lightly stir in the onions and a little seasoning. Leave to cool.

4. Cut the cheese into small cubes and halve the olives. Just before serving, finely chop the mint or parsley and stir into the rice together with the cheese and olives.

Warm Egg and Baby Potato Salad

Save time and washing up by cooking the potatoes and eggs in the same pan. Vary the dish by adding crispy bacon, diced ham, sliced cooked sausages, strips of smoked salmon, or lightly cooked asparagus spears.

Serves 2

1 small garlic clove
1 tbsp wine or cider vinegar
2 tsp wholegrain mustard
2 tsp clear honey
2 tbsp olive oil
Freshly milled salt and black pepper
4 spring onions
500g/1 lb 2 oz small new or salad potatoes
3 medium eggs
Salad leaves to serve

1. Crush the garlic into a small bowl or jug and whisk in the vinegar, mustard, honey and oil. Season lightly with salt and pepper.

2. Thinly slice the spring onions.

3. Halve the potatoes, put them in a saucepan and pour over sufficient boiling water to cover them. Add the eggs and bring just to the boil. Reduce the heat, cover and cook for 10 minutes.

4. Carefully lift out the eggs and stand them under cold running water. Re-cover the pan and continue cooking the potatoes for about 5–8 minutes or until tender.

5. When the eggs are cool enough to handle, peel off their shells and cut into quarters.

6. Drain the potatoes and tip them into a large bowl. Add the onions and half the dressing and toss gently until the potatoes are lightly coated.

7. To serve, pile the hot potatoes onto a bed of salad leaves and top with the eggs. Drizzle the remaining dressing over the eggs and serve.

Tabbouleh with Hot Salmon

Based on the Lebanese salad made with bulgur wheat (other-wise known as cracked wheat). Ask your fishmonger to skin the salmon. Alternatively, do it yourself: put the fish skin side down on a chopping board and, holding one end of the fish and keeping the sharp knife at a slight angle, slowly work the skin away from the flesh. Serve the salad with crusty bread.

Serves 4

125g/4½ oz bulgur wheat
350g/12 oz skinless salmon fillet
1 cucumber
6 tomatoes
4 spring onions
1 garlic clove
4 tbsp olive oil
2 tbsp lemon juice
3 tbsp freshly chopped mint
3 tbsp freshly chopped parsley
Freshly milled salt and pepper
55g/2 oz stoned black olives

1. Tip the bulgur wheat into a saucepan, cover with boiling water and boil for 10–12 minutes or until cooked and tender.

2. Meanwhile, slice the salmon into thin strips. Cut the cucumber in half lengthways and, with a small spoon, scoop out and discard the seeds. Finely chop the cucumber, tomatoes and spring onions. Crush the garlic.

3. Drain the cooked bulgur wheat in a fine sieve and rinse under running cold water. Then with the back of a spoon, press to squeeze out any excess water. Put into a clean bowl with the cucumber, tomatoes and spring onions.

4. Stir in 3 tbsp olive oil, the crushed garlic, lemon juice, chopped mint, parsley and seasoning. Cover and leave to stand for about 5–10 minutes to allow the flavours to infuse.

5. Meanwhile, heat a pan and pour in a little of the remaining oil. When hot add the salmon strips and cook over a high heat for 2–3 minutes until golden and cooked through.

6. Gently stir the cooked salmon and the olives into the tabbouleh and serve immediately.

Warm Tuna Salad with Nachos

Crushing the prawns intensifies the fish flavour. Instead of tomato juice, you could use tomato purée diluted with water and white wine vinegar in place of rice vinegar. It's important to assemble the salad ingredients before you start as tuna cooks very quickly.

Serves 4 as a starter or 2 as a main course

1 red onion
3 celery sticks
1 bunch of watercress
2 small fresh tuna steaks
4 tbsp olive oil
75g/2¾ oz cooked shelled prawns
1 tbsp tomato juice
1 tbsp Chinese rice wine vinegar
1 tsp lemon juice
2 tbsp freshly chopped dill
Freshly milled salt and pepper
Small bag of rocket leaves
Large bag of nachos

1. Cut the onion into very thin slices. Trim and slice the celery sticks. Roughly chop the watercress. Brush the tuna steaks on both sides with a little of the oil.

2. Very finely chop the prawns and mash with a fork or whizz with a stick blender. Scrape the crushed prawns and their juice into a small bowl. With a fork whisk in the remaining olive oil, tomato juice, vinegar, lemon juice and dill. Season to taste if necessary.

3. In a large salad bowl mix together the onion, celery, watercress and rocket leaves.

4. Meanwhile, heat a griddle or frying pan until very hot. Cook the tuna steaks very quickly on both sides until cooked on the outside but still pink inside (or a little longer if you prefer them cooked all the way through). Cut each steak into strips.

5. Quickly pour the dressing over the salad, add the tuna and gently mix the ingredients together. Serve immediately with nachos.

Hot Duck Salad

If time allows, leave the duck to marinate in the liquid for a couple of hours or in the fridge overnight. Try adding a little grated root ginger and/or some finely chopped fresh chilli to the marinade.

Serves 2

1 garlic clove
½ lemon
2 tbsp soy sauce
2 generous tsp clear honey
Freshly milled black pepper
2 boneless duck breasts
Mixed salad leaves

1. Crush the garlic and put into a shallow bowl (one that is just large enough to hold the two duck breasts in a single layer). Squeeze the juice from the lemon and add this to the bowl with the soy sauce, honey and pepper.

2. With a sharp knife, make several diagonal slashes in the fat of each duck breast (without cutting through into the meat). Add them to the mixture, turning to coat them well.

3. While you heat a non-stick frying pan, lift the duck out, reserving the liquid.

4. Add the duck, fat side down, to the hot pan and cook over a medium heat for about 2 minutes. When the fat side is a deep golden brown, turn the breasts over and cook the meat side for about 2 minutes until well browned. Lower the heat, flip the duck over onto the fat side again and continue cooking for about 10 minutes until it is done to your liking (cooking time will depend on the size and thickness of the duck breasts). Lift out and keep warm for 5–10 minutes to allow the meat to relax.

5. Meanwhile, drain off all but 1–2 tbsp fat from the pan. Add the reserved liquid and bubble for 1–2 minutes until slightly thickened, stirring in any crusty sediment from around the edges of the pan.

6. Slice the duck and scatter it over a plate of salad leaves. Drizzle the hot pan juices over the top and eat straight away.

Nutty Spiced Beef with Celeriac and Carrot

The flavours here are big and bold. It's a bit fiddly to make but well worth the effort.

Serves 4 as a starter or 2 as a main course

2 lean beef steaks, such as rump or fillet, about 350g/12 oz
    total weight
1 garlic clove
4 spring onions
Small piece of fresh root ginger
1 red chilli (see page 8)
1 tbsp olive oil
1 lemon
8 cherry tomatoes
Small bunch of coriander leaves
3 carrots
¼ celeriac, weighing about 225g/8 oz
4 slices of olive ciabatta
2 tbsp sweet chilli sauce
2 tsp horseradish sauce
1 tbsp walnut oil
150ml/¼ pint natural yogurt
Freshly milled black pepper
200g bag small salad leaves
Small handful of walnut pieces

1.   Trim any fat from the steaks and cut the meat into strips.

2.   Crush the garlic, slice the spring onions, peel and grate the ginger. Cut the chilli in half, remove and discard its seeds, and slice very thinly.

3.   Put the garlic, onions, ginger and chilli into a shallow bowl, stir in 2 tsp olive oil and the beef. Cover and leave to stand for 15 minutes or longer if time allows.

4.   Squeeze the juice from the lemon and pour into a large bowl. Quarter the tomatoes, chop the coriander, peel and grate the carrots and celeriac and mix all with the lemon juice (this prevents the celeriac browning). Cut the ciabatta into rough cubes.

5. In a small bowl mix together the sweet chilli sauce, horseradish sauce, walnut oil, yogurt and pepper.

6. While you heat a non-stick frying pan with the remaining olive oil, lift the beef out of its liquid with a slotted spoon. Reserve the marinade.

7. Add the beef to the hot pan and cook over a high heat for about 2 minutes until cooked to your liking. Add the reserved marinade and bubble for 1–2 minutes until slightly thickened.

8. Meanwhile heat another shallow pan until very hot, add the bread cubes and turn in the pan until crisp and piping hot.

9. Scatter the salad leaves in a large bowl and tip in the carrot and celeriac mixture. Add the hot beef and its juices, the crunchy bread and walnut pieces.

10 Pour the dressing over, mix quickly and eat straight away.

5

STRICTLY VEGETABLES

Both vegetarians and meat-eaters who are happy with an occasional non-meat meal will enjoy these strictly vegetable dishes. Of course, a little meat or fish can always be added to these recipes and, as one or two of them contain cheese, vegetarians will want to select the appropriate vegetarian versions.

In fact, these dishes are really adaptable. Sweet Potato and Beetroot Crush (opposite) or the Jumble of Vegetables with Toasted Cashews (on page 52), each delicious on its own, would also make ideal accompaniments to a main meat or fish course. Or try serving the Vegetables in Coconut Curry Sauce (page 54) or Red and White Bean Chilli (page 53) in a piping-hot, split baked potato, or on a bed of freshly cooked rice or pasta.

sweet potato and beetroot crush

Sweet Potato and Beetroot Crush with Parmesan

A pretty posh mash! The potatoes and beetroot are cooked in separate pans, then crushed and swirled together just before serving to give a stunning effect. Choose cooked beetroot that is not packed in vinegar. Wearing disposable gloves to prepare the beetroot will keep your hands stain free.

Serves 4–6

550g/1¼ lb sweet potatoes
2 cooked beetroots
1 orange
2 tsp vegetable bouillon
2 tbsp olive oil
2 tbsp grated Parmesan cheese
Freshly milled salt and black pepper

1. Peel and roughly chop the sweet potatoes and the beet-roots and put into separate pans. Finely grate the rind from the orange, cut in half and squeeze out the juice.

2. Sprinkle the bouillon over the sweet potatoes and cover with boiling water. Bring just to the boil, reduce the heat and cook gently for 6–8 minutes until soft, then drain.

3. Meanwhile, add the orange rind and juice to the beetroot and cook over a medium heat for a few minutes until piping hot and most of the liquid has reduced.

4. Pour the olive oil over the potatoes and crush with a fork, without mashing them to a purée. Stir in the Parmesan cheese and season if necessary.

5. Crush the beetroot with any remaining liquid in the pan.

6. Swirl the beetroot into the sweet potato mixture so that you can still see the different colours and serve immediately.

Mini Vegetables with Mushroom Purée

One to impress your friends – whole baby vegetables served with a smooth mushroom purée laced with brandy.

Serves 4

350g/12 oz chestnut mushrooms
3 shallots
1 garlic clove
450g/1 lb mini whole vegetables, such as carrots, corn,
    turnips, asparagus, leeks
2 tsp oil
25g/1 oz butter
1 tsp lemon juice
2 tsp brandy or milk
2 tbsp freshly chopped parsley
Freshly milled salt and black pepper

1. Clean, trim and slice the mushrooms and chop the shallots. Crush the garlic clove. Trim the mini vegetables.

2. Heat a small pan and add the oil and butter. Stir in the shallots and cook over a medium heat for about 5 minutes until softened. Stir in the mushrooms and garlic and cook quickly until browned, stirring frequently.

3. Add the lemon juice, brandy or milk, parsley and seasoning and cook for 2 minutes, stirring once or twice.

4. Remove from the heat and, with a stick blender or a food processor, whizz until smooth.

5. Meanwhile, cook the vegetables in a little boiling water for 6–8 minutes until just tender.

6. Serve the cooked vegetables with the mushroom purée.

Griddled Aubergines, Courgettes and Tomatoes with Mustard Croûtons

No griddle pan? Use an ordinary frying pan. A jar of chilli paste is useful to have in the fridge, though you could use 1–2 chopped fresh chillies instead (see page 8).

Serves 4

2 medium aubergines
3 courgettes
Olive oil
6 fresh plum tomatoes
3 tbsp wholegrain mustard
2 tsp chilli paste
2 tbsp tomato purée
25g/1 oz butter
2 tbsp sesame seeds
4 thick slices of bread

1. Trim the ends off the aubergines and courgettes, cut lengthways into slices and brush each side very lightly with oil. Cut the tomatoes in half. In a small bowl mix together the wholegrain mustard, chilli paste, tomato purée and butter.

2. Heat a griddle pan until very hot. Add some aubergine and courgette slices in a single layer and cook quickly for a few minutes until golden on both sides and cooked through. Lift out and keep warm. Cook the remaining slices. In the same hot pan, quickly brown the tomato halves on both sides.

3. Put the aubergine and courgette back into the pan, scatter the sesame seeds over and mix gently.

4. Meanwhile, make the croûtons. Heat the grill and toast the bread slices on one side. Turn the slices over and spread with the mustard mixture, grill until piping hot and cut into squares.

5. Serve the vegetables and tomatoes immediately with a few croûtons scattered over.

Corn, Carrot, and Courgette Fritters with Broad Bean Purée

It's worth making time to peel the outer skin off broad beans to reveal the beautiful green colour beneath. This dish is delicious served with soured cream in place of yogurt.

Serves 4

1 shallot
2 medium carrots
2 medium courgettes
2 medium potatoes
85g/3 oz sweetcorn
2 tsp plain flour
2 medium eggs
Freshly milled salt and black pepper
Oil, for frying
300ml/½ pint vegetable stock
1 tsp ground cumin
450g/1 lb broad beans
2 tbsp freshly chopped coriander
Thick Greek yogurt, to serve

1.   Finely chop the shallot. Coarsely grate the carrots, courgettes and potatoes. Mix all four vegetables together in a bowl, stir in the sweetcorn, flour and eggs, and season.

2.   Heat a little of the oil in a large frying pan. Drop three to four heaped spoonfuls of the vegetable mixture into the hot pan. Flatten a little with the back of a spoon and cook for 8–10 minutes, turning once, until cooked and golden. Carefully lift the fritters out of the pan and keep warm whilst you cook the remainder, adding more oil if necessary.

3.   Meanwhile, pour the stock into a pan, stir in the ground cumin and bring to the boil. Tip in the broad beans and cook for 10–12 minutes until soft.

4.   Using a stick blender whizz the broad beans and stock to a purée, stir in the coriander and season if necessary, then reheat.

5.   Spoon the bean purée onto plates and place one or two fritters on top. Serve immediately with yogurt.

Smoked Tofu and Vegetable Stir-Fry

Choose firm tofu rather than silken for this dish. If you can't find the smoked variety use plain instead – it will just taste different.

Serves 2

1 garlic clove
Small piece of fresh root ginger
4 tbsp soy sauce
2 tbsp dry sherry or stock
Pinch of ground Chinese five-spice or star anise
250g packet firm smoked tofu
1 small red onion
1 small carrot
2 tsp cornflour
1 tbsp oil
150g/5½ oz mange-touts
225g can sliced bamboo shoots
100g/3½ oz bean sprouts

1. Crush the garlic and grate the ginger into a bowl. Stir in the soy sauce, sherry or stock, and five-spice or star anise. Cut the tofu into bite-size cubes and stir into the mixture, coating it well.

2. Thinly slice the onion and carrot. With a slotted spoon, lift the tofu out of its liquid and reserve. Blend the cornflour with a little cold water to make a smooth paste and stir into the reserved liquid from the tofu.

3. Heat the oil in a wok or large frying pan. Add the tofu and cook quickly, stirring, for about 2 minutes until golden brown. Lift out with a slotted spoon and keep warm.

4. Add the onion, carrot and mange-touts to the pan and cook, stirring, for about 3 minutes, then add the bamboo shoots and bean sprouts and cook for another 2 minutes.

5. Pour the cornflour mixture over the vegetables and cook, stirring, until the sauce bubbles, thickens and coats the vegetables.

6. Serve the vegetables topped with the tofu.

A Jumble of Vegetables with Toasted Cashews

Make sure you use plain, unsalted cashews in this recipe, or you might like to try toasted almonds or pecans.

Serves 2

1 large onion
4 celery sticks
4 medium carrots
250g/9 oz broccoli florets
100g/3½ oz button mushrooms
50g/1¾ oz cashew nuts
2 tbsp olive oil
300ml/½ pint vegetable stock
142ml carton soured cream
1 tbsp cornflour
Freshly milled pepper

1. Thinly slice the onion, celery and carrots. Cut the broccoli into small florets and halve the mushrooms if large.

2. Tip the nuts into a medium frying pan and toast over a medium heat, stirring occasionally, until golden brown. Lift out and keep to one side.

3. Add the oil and onion to the pan and cook for about 5 minutes, stirring occasionally, until beginning to soften and turn golden brown.

4. Stir in the celery, carrots, broccoli and mushrooms. Cook for 2–3 minutes, stirring once or twice.

5. Add the stock and bring just to the boil, then cover and cook gently for about 10 minutes or until the vegetables are soft but still have a bite to them.

6. Meanwhile, blend the cream into the cornflour until smooth and season with pepper.

7. When the vegetables are ready, stir in the cream mixture and cook, stirring, until the sauce bubbles and thickens.

8. Serve the vegetables and sauce topped with the toasted cashews.

Red and White Bean Chilli

We use chilli paste here, but you could use any form of chilli you prefer – fresh, flaked or sauce – and adjust the quantity to suit your taste. For meat eaters, cook thin strips of chicken, beef or pork in a little oil in a separate pan and stir in. Serve it in bowls with some crusty bread, plain or garlicky, or as we have below, with yogurt and cheese.

Serves 4

1 medium onion
2 medium carrots
2 red peppers
2 garlic cloves
400g can cannellini beans
400g can red kidney beans
300ml/½ pint vegetable stock
2 tsp chilli paste
1 tbsp tomato purée
2 tsp sugar
1 tbsp oil
400g can plum or cherry tomatoes
Freshly milled salt and black pepper
Thick natural yogurt, to serve
Grated hard cheese, such as Cheddar, to serve

1. Thinly slice the onion and finely chop the carrots. Halve the peppers, remove and discard the seeds and stalk, and slice thinly. Crush or finely chop the garlic.
2. Drain and rinse the beans. Stir together the stock, chilli paste, tomato purée and sugar.
3. Heat the oil in a saucepan and stir in the onion, carrots and peppers. Cook over a medium heat for about 10 minutes, stirring frequently, until the vegetables are very soft and are just beginning to brown.
4. Stir in the garlic, followed by the beans and the tomatoes (if you are using plum tomatoes, cut them up roughly as they go into the pan). Add the stock mixture and a little seasoning.
5. Bring just to the boil, then cover and cook very gently for about 15 minutes, stirring occasionally.
6. Serve in bowls, topped with a generous spoonful of yogurt and some grated cheese.

Vegetables in Coconut Curry Sauce

Vary the vegetables and curry paste to suit your taste. For speed, serve with chapattis or naan bread. Alternatively, cook some basmati rice in a separate pan. And don't forget the mango chutney!

Serves 4

1 onion
1 aubergine
1 sweet potato
1 parsnip
Small piece of root ginger
400g can chickpeas
3 tbsp oil
1 tbsp curry paste
150ml/¼ pint vegetable stock
400g can chopped tomatoes
350ml/12 fl oz coconut milk

1. Thinly slice the onion. Cut the aubergine, sweet potato and parsnip into small cubes. Grate or finely chop the ginger. Drain the chickpeas.

2. Heat the oil in a large pan and add the onion, aubergine, sweet potato and parsnip. Cook over a medium heat for about 10 minutes, stirring occasionally, until beginning to soften and brown.

3. Add the ginger and curry paste and cook, stirring, for 1 minute.

4. Add the stock, chickpeas and tomatoes. Bring just to the boil, lower the heat, cover and cook gently for about 10 minutes or until the vegetables are tender.

5. Stir in the coconut milk, bring just to the boil and bubble gently for a minute or two before serving.

6

FASTA PASTA

Heaps of recipes can be made with pasta and noodles simply by adding a few flavourful ingredients. In our recipes we prefer to use dried pasta rather than fresh. The cooking times for dried pasta are slightly longer, but the results make this worthwhile.

Who would have thought that flour and water could be transformed into the weird and wonderful variety of pasta shapes? There's a shape for every sauce, and a sauce for every shape. Making the right match is the trick – just ask an Italian.

Smooth sauces are great with smooth shapes like spaghetti, tagliatelle, fettuccine and ribbon noodles. Chunky sauces are perfect for shells (conchiglie), twists (fusilli) or bows (farfalle) – all of which catch and hold the sauce. Then there are the flat lasagne sheets, ideal for making packets, like ravioli, to hold a filling.

You can find more pasta dishes in other chapters; see Pasta and Bacon in a Creamy Egg Sauce (page 94), Tomato and Orange Pasta Soup (page 29), and Large Pasta Triangles Filled with Crab and Prawns (page 90).

Linguine with a Creamy Nut Sauce

The ricotta makes a creamy sauce while the walnut pieces add a crunch. The anchovies cook down in the sauce to give a subtle flavour. Serve it with crusty bread.

Serves 4–6

2 shallots
2 garlic cloves
3 anchovy fillets
25g/1 oz pecorino or Parmesan cheese
1 tbsp olive oil
125g/4½ oz ricotta cheese
2 tbsp double cream
1 tbsp freshly chopped parsley
85g/3 oz walnut pieces
Freshly milled salt and pepper
350g/12 oz linguine pasta
1 tbsp vegetable bouillon

1. Finely chop the shallots and garlic. Chop the anchovy fillets. Grate the pecorino or Parmesan cheese.

2. Heat the olive oil in a medium pan, add the shallots and garlic and cook for a few minutes until softened. Reduce the heat, stir in the anchovy pieces and cook until they start to collapse and form a paste.

3. Add the ricotta cheese and sprinkle the pecorino or Parmesan cheese over, stirring until just melted. Mix in the double cream, chopped parsley, walnut pieces and seasoning if necessary. Don't let the sauce boil.

4. Meanwhile, cook the pasta following the packet instructions, adding the vegetable bouillon to the cooking water, and drain.

5. Gently stir the creamy sauce into the hot pasta and serve immediately.

Rainbow Pasta with Artichokes and Mushrooms

Simple is best! Flavoured pasta is now readily available in many shapes; the flavouring also gives the pasta its colour – spinach (green), beetroot and tomato (red) and squid ink (black). Toasted ciabatta bread goes well with this.

Serves 4–6

1 red onion
1 garlic clove
225g/8 oz button mushrooms
400g can artichoke hearts
Small bunch of fresh coriander
1 tbsp olive oil
350g/12 oz flavoured pasta shapes, choose a mix of
**   spinach, beetroot and tomato**
1 tbsp vegetable bouillon
1 tbsp sesame seed oil
Freshly milled salt and pepper

1. Thinly slice the onion. Crush or finely chop the garlic. Trim, clean and halve the mushrooms. Drain and quarter the artichoke hearts. Chop the coriander.

2. Heat the olive oil in a medium pan, add the onion and cook for a few minutes until softened. Add the garlic and mushroom halves and cook quickly, stirring once or twice, until golden.

3. Meanwhile, cook the pasta following the packet instructions, adding the vegetable bouillon to the cooking water, and drain.

4. Stir the artichoke hearts, coriander and sesame oil into the onion mixture and heat until the artichokes are piping hot. Season if necessary, stir into the hot pasta and serve immediately.

Pasta in Blue Cheese Sauce with Crisp Crumbs

A little well-flavoured cheese can go a long way. Try Dolcelatte, Cambozola, Gorgonzola or Stilton. It's good served with a salad of watercress, rocket and spinach.

Serves 2

1 small onion
100g/3½ oz blue cheese, such as Dolcelatte, Cambozola,
  Gorgonzola or Stilton
40g/1½ oz butter
50g/1¾ oz fresh breadcrumbs
175g/6 oz pasta shapes, such as penne, fusilli or shells
1 tbsp fresh thyme leaves
1 tsp plain flour
150ml/¼ pint milk
150ml/¼ pint vegetable stock
Freshly milled black pepper

1. Finely chop the onion and cut the cheese into small cubes.

2. In a small (preferably non-stick) frying pan, melt half the butter. Add the breadcrumbs and cook, stirring occasionally, until crisp and brown. Lift out and keep warm.

3. Cook the pasta following the packet instructions and drain.

4. Meanwhile, melt the remaining butter in the frying pan, add the onion and thyme leaves and cook over a medium heat, stirring occasionally, until the onion is soft but not brown. Stir in the flour and cook, stirring, for 1 minute. Remove from the heat and gradually stir in the milk, stock and cheese. Cook, stirring, until the sauce comes to the boil and thickens. Season with pepper.

5. Toss the drained pasta with the sauce and serve topped with the crisp crumbs.

Pasta with Mushrooms and Watercress

Good with British territorial cheeses, such as Red Leicester, Double Gloucester or Cheddar. Sometimes, we like to top the finished dish with crisp-fried bacon pieces.

Serves 2

2 shallots
400g/14 oz mixed mushrooms
50g/1¾ oz mature cheese, such as Red Leicester, Double Gloucester or Cheddar
175g/6 oz pasta shapes, such as penne or fusilli
2 tbsp olive oil
Freshly milled salt and black pepper
4 tbsp dry white wine or vermouth
200ml/7 fl oz vegetable stock
A handful of small watercress sprigs
1–2 tbsp finely chopped fresh parsley
1–2 tbsp chopped chives

1. Finely chop the shallots. Clean, trim and roughly chop the mushrooms. Finely grate the cheese.

2. Cook the pasta following the packet instructions and drain.

3. Meanwhile, heat a frying pan, add the oil and shallots and cook over a medium heat for a few minutes, stirring occasionally, until softened but not browned. Increase the heat, add the mushrooms and cook quickly for a few minutes until browned. Season with a little salt and pepper, then add the wine or vermouth and stock and bubble gently for 3–5 minutes.

4. Toss the mushroom mixture with the hot pasta, watercress and herbs.

5. Serve immediately with the cheese scattered over the top.

Pasta with Squash, Anchovies and Parmesan

Here's a simple list of ingredients with bold, exciting flavours that complement each other. Choose your favourite pasta shape – spirals, shells, bows or long ribbons of tagliatelle or spaghetti.

Serves 2

Wedge of butternut or acorn squash (see step 1 below)
A few fresh sage leaves
4 anchovy fillets
50g/1¾ oz Parmesan cheese
2 tbsp olive oil
175g/6 oz pasta (see note above)
Freshly milled salt and black pepper

1. Remove and discard the rind and seeds from the squash, and cut into small cubes, to make about 175g/6 oz finished weight.

2. Roughly chop the sage. Chop the anchovy fillets. Using a vegetable peeler, shave the Parmesan into thin flakes.

3. Heat a shallow pan, add the oil and squash and cook over a medium heat for about 5 minutes, stirring occasionally, until golden brown. Stir in the sage, cover, reduce the heat and cook gently for about 10 minutes or until the squash is just soft.

4. Meanwhile, cook the pasta following the packet instructions and drain.

5. Toss the hot pasta with the squash and the anchovy pieces.

6. Season if necessary and serve immediately with the Parmesan flakes scattered over the top.

Oriental Noodles with Spicy Prawns

Noodles, ginger, chilli, soy sauce and bean sprouts – a taste of the Orient. For a special occasion, use tiger prawns or even lobster meat.

Serves 4

4 spring onions
1 garlic clove
Small bunch of fresh coriander
Small piece of root ginger
1 red pepper
85g/3 oz mange-touts
Large handful of spinach leaves
350g/12 oz noodles
1 tbsp olive oil
350g/12 oz cooked shelled prawns
150ml/¼ pint chicken stock
2 tbsp sweet chilli sauce
Large handful of bean sprouts
1 tbsp soy sauce
Freshly milled salt and pepper
1 tbsp sesame seeds

1. Slice the spring onions, crush or finely chop the garlic and chop the coriander. Grate the root ginger. Halve the red pepper, remove and discard the seeds and stalk, and slice thinly. Cut the mange-touts in half diagonally. Tear the spinach leaves if they are large.

2. Cook the noodles following the packet instructions and drain.

3. Meanwhile, heat a wok or large frying pan, add the oil, spring onions, garlic and ginger, cook for a few seconds then add the prawns and red pepper and cook for 3 minutes.

4. Add the stock, sweet chilli sauce, mange-touts and spinach leaves. Bring just to the boil, stir in the bean sprouts, coriander and soy sauce.

5. Gently stir in the drained noodles, season if necessary, scatter the sesame seeds over then serve immediately.

Pasta with Salmon and Creamy Pesto Sauce

Using different pasta shapes, varying your choice of fish or using stock in place of wine will give endless variations to this simple recipe. Use other firm fish in place of salmon, such as tuna, swordfish or monkfish.

Serves 2

2 skinless salmon fillets
175g/6 oz pasta, such as tagliatelle, fettuccine or spaghetti
4 tbsp dry white wine or vermouth
1 tbsp pesto sauce
5–6 tbsp crème fraîche
Freshly milled salt and black pepper

1. Cut the salmon into strips about the size of your little finger.

2. Cook the pasta following the packet instructions and drain.

3. Meanwhile, heat a small non-stick frying pan and cook the salmon quickly until browned, then lift out. Add the white wine or vermouth to the pan and stir in the pesto and crème fraîche. Return the salmon to the pan and bubble the mixture gently for about 1 minute or until the salmon is just cooked through. Season if necessary.

4. Serve the pasta topped with the salmon and sauce.

Pasta Shells with Mince and Olive Sauce

Choose pasta shells for this recipe, which is based on a traditional Italian dish. Also called conchiglie, their shape is perfect for holding the delicious meat and tomato sauce. Serve with crusty bread.

Serves 4

1 large onion
2 garlic cloves
100g/3½ oz mushrooms
8 pitted green olives
2 tsp olive oil
225g/8 oz lean minced beef
200g can chopped tomatoes
1 beef stock cube
3 tbsp tomato purée
1 tbsp lemon juice
Freshly milled salt and pepper
350g/12 oz pasta shells
1 tbsp vegetable bouillon
Basil leaves

1. Thinly slice the onion. Crush or finely chop the garlic. Trim, clean and slice the mushrooms. Quarter the olives.

2. Heat the oil in a medium pan, add the onion and cook for a few minutes until softened. Add the minced beef, garlic and mushroom slices, cook until browned, breaking up the mince with a spoon.

3. Pour in the tomatoes and 150ml/¼ pint cold water and add the stock cube, tomato purée, olives and lemon juice. Bring just to the boil, then lower the heat and cook gently for 15 minutes. Season if necessary.

4. Meanwhile, cook the pasta shells following the packet instructions, adding the vegetable bouillon to the cooking water, and drain.

5. Serve the hot pasta with the sauce spooned over and basil leaves scattered on top.

7

STARRING RICE & GRAINS

Every day it's bread and potatoes – do you sometimes feel stuck in a rut? If so, it's time to explore the realms of rice and grains. Each type of grain and rice has its own distinctive flavour and texture, and each one can be put to use in diverse and interesting ways.

Some grains, like couscous and bulgur wheat, are superb at soaking up flavours from sauces and dressings. Cornmeal (polenta) is very versatile – it can be served smooth and soft, like mashed potatoes, or firm enough to be sliced and grilled or fried.

Rice is a star turn for all occasions. A fluffy pile of rice goes well with a sauce; for meat dishes, a fragrant or spiced rice mixture is often a must; and then there is the creamy rice of a nourishing risotto.

There are rice dishes in other chapters as well – see Paella (on page 75), Chicken Pilaff (page 77) and Savoury Salmon Rice (page 13).

rice... a star turn for all occasions

Polenta with Cheese and Vegetables

Polenta, made from cornmeal, hails from Northern Italy. It can be eaten hot with a little butter or cooled until firm, cut into squares and fried or grilled or oven baked. Here it is mixed with cheese and served, still soft, like mashed potato.

Serves 4

2 medium onions
1 garlic clove
1 red pepper
175g/6 oz fresh plum tomatoes
100g/3½ oz sugar-snap peas
175g/6 oz Cheddar cheese
280g/10 oz coarse-grain polenta
1 tbsp olive oil
50g/1¾ oz sweetcorn
2 tsp vegetable bouillon
Freshly milled salt and black pepper
2 tbsp grated Parmesan cheese
2 tbsp freshly chopped coriander leaves

1. Thinly slice the onions. Crush or finely chop the garlic. Cut the pepper in half, remove and discard the seeds and stalk, and chop roughly. Dice the tomatoes and cut the sugar-snap peas in half. Grate the Cheddar cheese.

2. Cook the polenta following the packet instructions until very thick.

3. Meanwhile, heat the oil in a medium pan, add the onions and cook over a medium heat for a few minutes, stirring occasionally, until just beginning to soften.

4. Stir in the garlic, pepper, sweetcorn and tomatoes and cook for 2 minutes. Pour in 150ml/¼ pint boiling water and the vegetable bouillon. Cook for 6–8 minutes, stirring occasionally, until the sweetcorn is soft. Add the sugar-snap peas and cook for 1 minute. Season if necessary.

5. Into the hot polenta, stir the two cheeses and the coriander leaves.

6. Spoon the polenta onto warmed serving plates, make a well in the centre and spoon in the vegetable mixture.

Mixed Mushroom and Red Onion Risotto

Risotto is made using short grain Italian rice such as arborio, carnaroli or vialone nano. When cooked, the grains should retain a slight bite while the finished result is moist and porridge like.

Serves 4

15g/½ oz dried wild porcini mushrooms
1 medium red onion
1 garlic clove
175g/6 oz mixed fresh mushrooms, such as chestnut,
   oyster, shiitake
4 fresh sage leaves
600ml/1 pint light vegetable or chicken stock or a mixture
2 tbsp olive oil
250g/9 oz risotto rice, such as carnaroli
150ml/¼ pint dry red wine
Freshly milled salt and black pepper
3 tbsp freshly grated Parmesan cheese, plus extra for
   serving
25g/1 oz butter, cut into small cubes
2 tbsp finely chopped fresh parsley

1. Put the dried mushrooms into a bowl, pour 300ml/½ pint boiling water over them and leave to stand while you prepare the vegetables.
2. Meanwhile, finely chop the onion and garlic. Clean, trim and chop the fresh mushrooms. Tear the sage leaves.
3. Drain the soaked mushrooms, reserving the liquid, and chop finely. Put the reserved liquid into a saucepan, add the stock, bring the mixture just to the boil, reduce the heat and keep hot.
4. Put the oil, onion and garlic into a large pan and cook over a medium heat for 5–10 minutes, stirring frequently, until soft but not browned.
5. Add the rice and cook, stirring, for about 2 minutes. Stir in the fresh mushrooms, the chopped dried mushrooms and the sage leaves. Add the wine and cook, stirring, until absorbed.
6. Stirring continuously, add the hot stock, a ladleful at a time and waiting until the liquid has been absorbed before the next addition, until the rice is cooked and creamy but still retains a slight bite. Expect this to take about 20 minutes.
7. Season lightly and stir in the Parmesan cheese, butter and parsley. Serve topped with extra Parmesan.

Quinoa with Chickpeas and Spring Vegetables

Quinoa was a staple of the ancient Incas who knew it as 'the mother grain'. The tiny, bead-shape grains have a delicate flavour and are cooked like rice. Don't expect them to soften completely; they will retain a slight bite.

Serves 2

1 small onion
1 garlic clove
1 red pepper
425g can chickpeas
150g/5½ oz quinoa
300ml/½ pint vegetable stock
1 tbsp cider vinegar or wine vinegar
1 tbsp olive oil
1 tsp sweet chilli sauce (optional)
Handful of sugar-snap peas
Handful of young asparagus tips
Small handful of chopped fresh parsley
Freshly milled black pepper

1. Finely chop the onion and the garlic. Halve the pepper, remove and discard the seeds and stalk, and slice thinly. Drain the chickpeas.

2. Put the quinoa and stock into a saucepan, bring just to the boil, cover and cook gently for 12–15 minutes until the grain is tender (it will retain a slight crunch) and the liquid has been absorbed. Stir in the vinegar.

3. Meanwhile, put the oil into a saucepan and add the onion. Cook over a medium heat for about 5 minutes, stirring occasionally, until beginning to soften but not brown. Add the garlic and red pepper and cook for 2–3 minutes, stirring occasionally. Add the chickpeas, chilli sauce (if using) and 3 tbsp water. Cover and cook gently for 2–3 minutes. Add the peas and asparagus, cover and cook for about 3 minutes.

4. Stir the hot quinoa into the hot vegetable mixture with the parsley and season lightly with pepper.

5. Serve immediately.

Buckwheat with Mushrooms and Mozzarella

The triangular seeds called buckwheat are actually a herb. They have an assertive flavour and are cooked in the same way as rice. Here, we use the unroasted version.

Serves 4

6 spring onions
350g/12 oz mushrooms
125g/4½ oz mozzarella cheese
200g/7 oz unroasted buckwheat
1 vegetable stock cube
2 tsp oil
2 tbsp single cream
1 tbsp lemon juice
2 tbsp freshly chopped parsley
Freshly milled salt and black pepper

1. Finely chop the spring onions. Clean, trim and roughly chop the mushrooms. Cut the mozzarella cheese into small cubes.

2. Pour the buckwheat into a medium pan and cook following the packet instructions, adding the stock cube to the cooking water and draining if necessary.

3. Meanwhile, heat the oil in a frying pan, add the onions and chopped mushrooms and cook for a few minutes until softened and golden brown.

4. Tip the onions and mushrooms into the pan of cooked buckwheat. Over a low heat stir in the cream, lemon juice and chopped parsley.

5. Season to taste and serve immediately.

Surf 'n' Turf with Coconut Rice

Meat and fish together in one dish. Why not buy a bag of frozen mixed seafood and use a handful for this recipe?

Serves 4

1 medium onion
1 garlic clove
Small piece of root ginger
350g/12 oz boneless chicken breast
250g/9 oz long grain rice
Half a 400ml can coconut milk
1 tbsp oil
175g/6 oz mixed cooked shelled seafood, such as prawns,
  cockles, clams, shrimps
150ml/¼ pint chicken stock
1 tbsp soy sauce
125g/4½ oz peas
Large handful of coriander leaves
Freshly milled black pepper

1. Thinly slice the onion. Crush or finely chop the garlic. Peel and finely grate the ginger.

2. Cut the chicken into bite-size pieces.

3. Cook the rice following the packet instructions, replacing some of the water with the coconut milk, and drain.

4. Meanwhile, heat the oil in a frying pan, add the onion and cook over a medium heat for a few minutes, stirring occasionally, until just beginning to soften.

5. Stir in the garlic. Increase the heat, add the chicken and cook, stirring occasionally, until golden brown and just cooked through.

6. Add the seafood, chicken stock, ginger, soy sauce and peas. Cook, stirring occasionally, for 2–3 minutes until cooked through. Stir in the coriander leaves and season if necessary.

7. Spoon the rice onto warmed plates, top with the chicken and seafood mixture and serve immediately.

Couscous with Vegetables, Chicken, Lime and Coriander

Couscous appears in traditional North African dishes and is made from semolina or cracked wheat. Serve this dish warm on the day it is made; any left over can be put in the fridge and served the next day.

Serves 2

1 medium leek
1 medium carrot
1 celery stick
1 garlic clove
1 lime
Handful of cherry tomatoes
1 large boneless chicken breast
2 tbsp olive oil
300ml/½ pint vegetable stock
125g/4½ oz couscous
Freshly milled salt and pepper
Handful of chopped fresh coriander

1. Thinly slice the leek, carrot and celery. Finely chop or crush the garlic. Finely grate the rind from the lime, half and squeeze out the juice. Halve the tomatoes. Cut the chicken into thin strips.

2. Put half the oil into a saucepan (preferably non-stick) and add the leek, carrot and celery. Cook over a medium heat for about 5 minutes, stirring occasionally, until beginning to soften but not brown.

3. Increase the heat, add the chicken and cook for a few minutes until the contents of the pan begin to turn golden brown.

4. Add the garlic, tomatoes, lime rind and juice and stock. Bring just to the boil, stir in the couscous and remove from the heat. Cover and leave to stand for 10 minutes until all the liquid has been absorbed.

5. Using a fork, fluff up the couscous, stirring in a little seasoning if necessary, the coriander and the remaining oil.

Spiced Couscous with Turkey and Okra

In this recipe, the delicate grains of couscous pick up the flavours of the ginger, cumin and lime.

Serves 4–6

1 medium red onion
1 garlic clove
1 small lime
175g/6 oz okra
2 medium carrots
½ pomegranate (optional)
450g/1 lb boneless turkey breast
1 tbsp plain flour
350g/12 oz couscous
2 tsp vegetable bouillon
1 tbsp oil
300ml/½ pint turkey or chicken stock
Small handful of sultanas
1 tsp ground ginger
1 tsp ground cumin
3 tbsp freshly chopped parsley
Freshly milled salt and black pepper
1 tbsp pine nuts

1. Thinly slice the onion. Crush or finely chop the garlic. Finely grate the rind from the lime, halve and squeeze out the juice. Trim the okra and, if large, cut in half crossways. Slice the carrots. With a small spoon scrape out and reserve the seeds from the pomegranate. Dice the turkey and dust in the flour.

2. Cook the couscous following the packet instructions, adding the vegetable bouillon to the cooking water.

3. Meanwhile, heat the oil in a frying pan, add the onion and cook over a medium heat for a few minutes, stirring occasionally, until just beginning to soften. Stir in the garlic. Increase the heat, add the turkey and cook quickly, stirring occasionally, until golden brown.

4. Stir in the stock, carrots, okra, sultanas, ground ginger and cumin, lime rind and lime juice. Bring just to the boil, reduce the heat and cook gently for about 15 minutes until the turkey is cooked through.

5. Stir the parsley and hot couscous into the pan, add a little seasoning if wished and gently stir it all together.

6. Serve immediately, sprinkled with pine nuts and pomegranate seeds if using.

Rice with Spiced Lamb

This simple dish is equally good made with beef steak or chicken in place of the lamb. Use your favourite curry powder or paste and adjust the quantities to suit your taste.

Serves 2

1 medium onion
1 garlic clove
1 small lemon
About 6 ready-to-eat dried apricots
350g/12 oz lamb fillet
2–3 tsp curry powder
125g/4½ oz long grain rice, such as basmati
1 tsp vegetable bouillon
2 tsp oil
Freshly milled salt and black pepper
2 tbsp toasted flaked almonds

1. Thinly slice the onion. Crush or finely chop the garlic. Finely grate the rind from the lemon, halve and squeeze out the juice. Cut the apricots into small pieces. Thinly slice the lamb and toss the slices in the curry powder.

2. Cook the rice following the packet instructions, adding the vegetable bouillon to the cooking water, and drain, reserving a little of the liquid.

3. Meanwhile, heat the oil in a frying pan, add the onion and cook over a medium heat for a few minutes, stirring occasionally, until just beginning to soften. Stir in the garlic. Increase the heat, add the lamb and cook quickly, stirring occasionally, until golden brown and just cooked through. Remove from the heat and stir in the apricots, lemon rind and lemon juice.

4. Tip the hot rice into a warmed serving dish and add the lamb mixture. Rinse the frying pan with 2–3 tbsp of the liquid reserved from the rice, and drizzle it over the lamb. Add a little seasoning if wished and gently stir the whole lot together.

5. Serve immediately, sprinkled with toasted almonds.

8

TAKE ONE BIG SHALLOW PAN

Use just one burner and just one pan. All these recipes are cooked in a large, shallow pan, a frying pan or a wok. Take the pan to the table and serve the meal from there. These dishes are great for students with rudimentary cooking facilities, and also a boon for everyone to save on the washing up.

These are ideal weekday meals, but equally good and impressive enough to share with friends at the weekend or at any time. In a convivial atmosphere, with the pan sizzling at the centre of the dinner table, pour out the wine and enjoy!

two-course fish soup

Two-Course Fish Soup

Based on a dish Norma tasted in Spain, this is a two-course meal from one pan. And it's back to front! The main course is served before the soup.

Serves 4

2 medium potatoes
1 large onion
2 garlic cloves
2 green peppers
1 lemon
Small bunch of parsley
450g/1 lb mixed fish fillets, such as trout, salmon, sole, plaice, haddock
2 tbsp olive oil
600ml/1 pint fish stock
400g can tomatoes
Pinch of saffron threads (optional)
Freshly milled salt and black pepper
Crusty bread, to serve

1. Peel and thinly slice the potatoes and put into a bowl of cold water to remove some of the starch. Chop the onion and crush the garlic. Cut the peppers in half, remove and discard the seeds and stalk, and dice roughly. Grate the rind from the lemon, cut in half and squeeze the juice. Chop the parsley. Cut each fish fillet into four.
2. Heat the oil in a large, shallow pan, add the onion and garlic and cook gently for a few minutes until softened. Arrange the fish fillets on top, skin side down, and cook quickly until the skin has browned. Lift out of the pan.
3. Drain the potato slices. Increase the heat under the pan and pour in the fish stock and tomatoes. Bring to the boil, stir in the potato slices and cook for 6 minutes (it doesn't matter if the slices begin to break as they cook).
4. Sprinkle in the saffron threads (if using), parsley, lemon rind and juice. Add the peppers and season. Reduce the heat, add the fish fillets and cook gently for 6–8 minutes or until the fish is cooked.
5. Serve from the pan in wide, shallow bowls. With a slotted spoon, lift out the fish and vegetables and eat these first. Then, with a ladle, serve the rest as soup with crusty bread.

Paella

Try not to stir the paella during cooking (unless it threatens to burn) and you will achieve a lovely crust at the bottom.

Serves 4

1 onion
2 garlic cloves
1 red pepper
1 green pepper
2 tomatoes
Small bunch of parsley
50g/1¾ oz chorizo or spicy sausage
4 skinless boneless chicken thighs
About 300g/10½ oz skinless white fish
4 tbsp olive oil
400g paella rice or risotto rice
1 litre/1¾ pint chicken stock
Freshly milled black pepper
Pinch of saffron threads
About 12 mussels in their shells
About 12 raw tiger prawns in their shells

1. Finely chop the onion and garlic. Halve the peppers, remove and discard the seeds and stalks, and chop roughly. Chop the tomatoes and the parsley. Slice the sausage. Cut each chicken thigh into about four pieces. Cut the fish into bite-size pieces.

2. Put the oil, onion and garlic into a large, shallow pan and cook gently for 5–10 minutes, stirring occasionally, until softened but not browned.

3. Add the chicken, increase the heat and cook for a few minutes until lightly browned.

4. Stir in the peppers and tomatoes. Add the rice and cook, stirring, for a minute or two.

5. Stir in the sausage, stock, black pepper and saffron and bring just to the boil. Reduce the heat and cook very gently (uncovered and preferably without stirring) for about 20 minutes or until the rice is just cooked and the liquid has been absorbed.

6. Add the fish and shellfish and continue cooking for about 5 minutes or until just cooked through.

7. Serve immediately, sharing out the delicious crusty bits from the bottom of the pan and sprinkling with plenty of chopped parsley.

Chilli Chicken

This is the dish on the front cover of this book. It's colourful, it's simple and it's quick. Serve it with crusty bread.

Serves 4

2 small red onions
1 red pepper
1 orange pepper
2 medium courgettes
175g/6 oz mixed mushrooms
450g/1 lb boneless chicken
2 tbsp olive oil
1 tsp mild chilli powder
300ml/½ pint chicken stock
Small spinach leaves
Freshly milled salt and pepper

1. Quarter the red onions and slice thinly. Cut the peppers in half, remove and discard the seeds and stalks, and slice thinly. Trim and slice the courgettes. Clean and trim the mushrooms, slicing them if large.

2. Cut the chicken into thin strips.

3. Heat the oil in a large, shallow pan and add the onions, peppers, courgettes and mushrooms. Cook quickly for a few minutes, stirring occasionally, until golden. Lift out of the pan and keep warm.

4. If necessary add a little more oil to the pan and heat. Add the chicken strips, a few at a time, and cook quickly until golden. Lift out of the pan, keep warm and cook the remaining chicken.

5. Return the vegetables and chicken to the pan, sprinkle the chilli over and add the stock. Bring just to the boil, reduce the heat and cook gently for 10–15 minutes or until the chicken is cooked throughout, adding the spinach leaves for the final 2 minutes.

6. Season if necessary and serve immediately.

Chicken Pilaff with Saffron Yogurt

A pilaff always involves browning the rice in oil or butter before cooking it gently in stock. This one is accompanied by a pretty saffron-yellow yogurt. Sometimes chicken thighs are sold with excess fat and skin attached – if so, do trim them.

Serves 4

Pinch of saffron threads
142ml carton natural yogurt
Freshly milled salt and pepper
1 small onion
100g/3½ oz button mushrooms
8 chicken thighs with skin on
1 tbsp oil
250g/9 oz long grain rice
600ml/1 pint chicken stock
50g/1¾ oz toasted flaked almonds

1. Stir the saffron threads into the yogurt, season with a little salt and pepper and put to one side.

2. Thinly slice the onion and halve the mushrooms. Trim any excess fat and skin from the chicken.

3. Heat the oil in a large, non-stick frying pan, add the chicken and cook over a high heat, turning occasionally, until golden brown. Lift out and drain on kitchen paper. Pour off any excess fat from the pan, leaving 1–2 tbsp behind.

4. To the hot pan, add the onion and mushrooms and cook quickly, stirring, until beginning to brown.

5. Stir in the rice and cook, stirring, for 1–2 minutes until lightly browned, making sure it does not burn.

6. Add the stock and the chicken, pushing the pieces under the liquid.

7. Bring just to the boil, reduce the heat, cover and cook gently for 15–20 minutes, stirring once or twice, until the rice is tender, the stock has been absorbed and the chicken is cooked through.

8. Serve topped with the saffron yogurt and toasted flaked almonds.

Thai Coconut Curried Meatballs

Thai curries are light, fragrant and often flavoured with coconut. We've used green Thai curry paste (buy it in small jars) but red paste would make a delicious alternative. Serve with warm pitta bread or hot rice.

Serves 4

1 small onion
1 garlic clove
1 green pepper
6 large tomatoes
2 pak choi
350g/12 oz minced chicken
Freshly milled pepper
Plain flour
1 tbsp olive oil
2 tbsp green Thai curry paste
150ml/¼ pint coconut milk
150ml/¼ pint chicken stock
1 tbsp lime juice
2 tbsp freshly chopped coriander

1. Finely chop the onion and crush the garlic clove. Cut the pepper in half, remove and discard the seeds and stalk, and slice thinly. Roughly chop the tomatoes. Separate the pak choi leaves, breaking the larger ones in half.

2. In a medium bowl put the onion, garlic and minced chicken. Season with pepper and mix with a fork. With wetted hands shape spoonfuls of the mixture into balls. Dust them with a little flour.

3. Heat the oil in a large, shallow pan, add the meatballs and cook quickly until golden all over. Lift out of the pan.

4. Increase the heat, add the curry paste to the pan then stir in the coconut milk, chicken stock and lime juice. Bring just to the boil, reduce the heat and cook gently for 2 minutes.

5. Return the meatballs to the pan, add the tomatoes and green pepper and cook on a medium heat for 10–15 minutes or until the chicken is cooked through, adding the pak choi for the final 2 minutes.

6. Scatter the coriander over and serve.

Pork 'Burgers' with Watercress and Pine Nuts

Who says burgers have to be round? This one is pan size and cut into wedges just before serving. Let your family and friends customise theirs by offering them a selection of breads, salad leaves, chutneys and sauces.

Serves 4

2 large onions
1 garlic clove
4 sun-dried tomatoes
6 ready-to-eat dried apricots
1 bunch of watercress
6 fresh sage leaves
50g/1¾ oz pine nuts
1 green eating apple
450g/1 lb minced lean pork
1 tbsp soy sauce
Freshly milled salt and pepper
Olive oil

To serve:
4 burger buns or pitta breads
Salad leaves
Pickles, mayonnaise, mustard and ketchup

1. Finely chop the onions and crush the garlic. Finely chop the sun-dried tomatoes, apricots, watercress, sage leaves and pine nuts. Peel and quarter the apple, remove and discard the core, and chop finely.
2. Put all these ingredients in a large bowl. Add the minced pork and soy sauce and season well. With your hands, mix well.
3. Brush the base of a wide, shallow non-stick pan with a little oil and add the pork mixture, pressing it out into a large thick burger. Cook over a medium heat until the pork is golden brown on the bottom.
4. Remove the pan from the heat and carefully slide the burger out onto a flat plate. Carefully slide it back into the pan, browned side up.
5. Continue cooking until the pork is cooked throughout.
6. Cut into wedges and serve in buns or pitta breads. Add your choice of salad leaves, pickles, mayonnaise, mustard and ketchup.

9

IT'S A WRAP

Wrap it up and take it with you! More exciting than a sandwich, wraps are the funkiest food for people on the go. Buy the wraps and make the fillings yourself. With plenty to choose from – pitta breads or flat breads, soft tortillas, naan bread or pancakes – you can improvise at will. The fillings, like Hot Chilli Beef (on page 88) or Tuna and Avocado (page 83), can be hot and spicy; or like Garlic and Lime Prawns (page 82) light and cool; or like Salmon with Peppers and Onion (page 84) rich and filling. There are endless filling-and-wrap combinations, many of them interchangeable.

The recipes include suggestions for the best wraps to use. To heat them, either follow the instructions on the packet or find your own clever way to warm them up for serving. Why not wrap them securely in foil and pop them under the grill? Or sit the parcel on top of the pan in which the filling is cooking. Or stack them on a plate, cover with foil and sit atop a small pan of gently bubbling water. Or put them on a plate, cover with film and heat in the microwave on medium power until warmed through.

Courgette, Sweetcorn and Two Cheeses

The sauce is made with the all-in-one method – milk, butter and flour goes into a pan and, so long as you keep stirring with a whisk, you'll have a lump-free sauce.

Serves 4

2 medium courgettes
4 spring onions
60g/2¼ oz mature Red Leicester cheese
60g/2¼ oz mature Cheddar cheese
150ml/¼ pint natural yogurt
1 tbsp smooth chutney
Freshly milled salt and pepper
2 tsp oil
75g/2¾ oz sweetcorn
600ml/1 pint milk
50g/1¾ oz butter
50g/1¾ oz plain flour
2 tsp wholegrain mustard
4 soft corn tortilla wraps

1. Trim and finely chop the courgettes and thinly slice the spring onions. Grate the Red Leicester and Cheddar cheeses.

2. Pour the yogurt into a bowl, stir in the chutney and season to taste. Cover and chill until needed.

3. Heat the oil in a frying pan, add the courgettes and spring onions and cook gently until they begin to soften. Stir in the sweetcorn and remove from the heat.

4. Pour the milk into a medium pan, add the butter and flour. Beating with a whisk (preferably a coil type), bring to the boil and cook gently for 3–5 minutes until thickened and smooth.

5. Stir in the grated cheeses, wholegrain mustard and the courgette mixture. Stirring continuously, cook until the cheese has melted.

6. Heat the tortillas (see opposite). Spoon the filling onto one tortilla, and then fold it over the filling. Repeat with the remaining tortillas and filling and serve with the flavoured yogurt to spoon over.

Garlic and Lime Prawns in Traditional Pancakes

A stylish wrap that can be served just as it is or sliced as an elegant starter. When buying pancakes, choose the unsweetened variety. We also like the prawn mixture stuffed into pitta breads.

Serves 4

2 cabbage leaves
2 red chillies (see page 8)
2 garlic cloves
1 small lime
1 tbsp olive oil
2 tsp sesame seed oil
350g/12 oz cooked shelled large prawns, thawed if frozen
2 tbsp fish stock
3 tbsp freshly chopped parsley
2 tsp sesame seeds
Freshly milled salt and pepper
8 ready-made traditional pancakes
Plain yogurt and lime wedges, to serve

1. Finely shred the cabbage leaves. Halve the chillies, remove and discard the seeds, and slice thinly. Crush the garlic cloves. With a potato peeler remove the rind from half the lime without removing the white pith and cut into shreds. Squeeze the juice from the whole lime.
2. Heat a saucepan and add a little of the olive oil. Carefully add the shredded cabbage (it may splatter) and cook over a high heat for a few seconds until crisp. With a slotted spoon lift onto kitchen paper to drain.
3. Pour the remaining olive oil and the sesame seed oil into the pan and when hot add the chillies, lime rind and crushed garlic. Cook for a minute to extract the flavours.
4. Add the prawns and cook over a high heat for 2–3 minutes until the prawns begin to brown a little.
5. Add the fish stock and lime juice, and cook until the mixture bubbles. Stir in the chopped parsley and sesame seeds and season to taste with salt and pepper.
6. Heat the pancakes (see page 80). Spoon the filling onto the pancakes and roll or fold over. Serve with yogurt and lime wedges to squeeze over.

Tuna and Avocado Pitta Breads

We have used canned tuna – try salmon or mackerel for a change. It's a soft mixture that also makes a lovely filling for ready-made pancakes.

Serves 4

1 small red onion
6 cherry tomatoes
200g can tuna chunks in brine
½ small cos lettuce
Bunch of radishes
1 large avocado
1 tbsp lemon juice
1 tsp olive oil
1 tsp mild curry paste
Freshly milled salt and pepper
4 pitta breads
150ml/¼ pint crème fraîche

1. Thinly slice the red onion and quarter the cherry tomatoes. Drain the tuna. Finely shred the lettuce and slice the radishes.

2. Halve the avocado, remove and discard the stone. Scoop out the flesh and roughly chop. Put into a small bowl and stir in the lemon juice to prevent browning. Cover and chill.

3. Heat a saucepan and add the oil, curry paste and sliced red onion. Cook over a medium heat for a few minutes, stirring once or twice, until the onion has softened.

4. Add the drained tuna and gently stir into the curried onion mixture. Remove from the heat and season if necessary.

5. Heat the pitta breads (see page 80). Cut each pitta bread in half and open up to make pockets. Half fill each pocket with shredded lettuce, sliced radishes, tomato quarters and avocado. Spoon in the curried tuna mixture and add a blob of crème fraîche.

Salmon with Peppers and Onion

Rich, filling and colourful – serve it with a crisp green salad.

Serves 4–6

1 red pepper
6 spring onions
Handful of mange-touts
About 600g/1 lb 5 oz skinless boneless salmon fillet
2 tbsp olive oil
40g/1½ oz plain flour
450ml/16 fl oz milk
Freshly milled salt and pepper
8–12 ready-made traditional pancakes

1. Halve the pepper, remove and discard its seeds and stalk, and slice thinly. Thinly slice the spring onions. Slice the mange-touts thickly on the diagonal. Cut the salmon into bite-size cubes.

2. Heat a saucepan and add the oil, red pepper and spring onions. Cook over a medium heat for a few minutes until the pepper just begins to soften without browning.

3. Remove from the heat and stir in the flour, then gradually stir in the milk.

4. Slowly heat the sauce, stirring continuously, until it comes to the boil and thickens. Season lightly with salt and pepper.

5. Add the salmon and mange-touts and cook gently for a few minutes until the fish is just cooked.

6. Heat the pancakes (see page 80). Spoon the mixture onto the pancakes, roll up and serve.

Satay Chicken

We use crunchy peanut butter for its texture – use the smooth version if you prefer. Annette likes simply to pile the mixture onto flatbreads.

Serves 2

1 small onion
1 garlic clove
2 boneless, skinless chicken breasts
1 tbsp oil
1 tsp sugar
¼ tsp chilli powder
100ml/3½ fl oz coconut milk
3 generous tbsp crunchy peanut butter
Freshly milled salt and black pepper
½ lemon

1. Finely chop the onion. Crush or finely chop the garlic. Thinly slice the chicken.

2. Heat half the oil in a non-stick frying pan and add the chicken. Cook over a medium-high heat, stirring occasionally, until golden brown and cooked through. Lift out.

3. Add the remaining oil to the pan and add the onion and sugar. Cook gently for 5–8 minutes, stirring occasionally, until very soft and beginning to turn golden brown.

4. Add the garlic and chilli to the onion and cook, stirring, for a minute or two.

5. Stir in the coconut milk and peanut butter and heat gently, stirring, until the mixture comes to the boil. Add the chicken and bubble gently for a minute or two until the chicken is heated through, seasoning with a little salt and pepper if necessary.

6. Just before serving, squeeze over lemon juice to taste.

7. Heat your chosen wraps (see page 80), fill and serve.

Chicken with Orange and Honey Glaze

This works well with sliced lean pork too. Choose your favourite wraps – flatbreads, pitta breads, soft tortillas, naan bread, chapattis, parathas or pancakes – adding plenty of crisp salad leaves.

Serves 2

1 small orange
Small piece of fresh root ginger
2 tsp soy sauce
2 tsp clear honey
1 tsp cornflour
4 spring onions
2 boneless, skinless chicken breasts
1 tbsp oil

1. Finely grate the orange rind, halve and squeeze out the juice. Finely grate enough ginger to make about 1 tsp. Combine the orange rind and juice with the ginger, soy sauce, honey and cornflour, mixing well.

2. Slice the spring onions. Thinly slice the chicken.

3. Heat the oil in a frying pan. Add the chicken and cook quickly, stirring occasionally, until golden brown and cooked through.

4. Remove the pan from the heat and add the spring onions. Stir the orange mixture and add it to the pan. Return the pan to the heat and, stirring continuously, heat quickly until the sauce bubbles, thickens and coats the chicken.

5. Heat your chosen wraps (see page 80), fill and serve.

Lamb with Yogurt, Herb and Mustard Dressing

Again, choose your favourite wraps – flatbreads, pitta breads, soft tortillas, naan bread, chapattis, parathas or pancakes – adding shredded lettuce and maybe some tomato or cucumber slices.

Serves 2–3

200g carton Greek yogurt
1 heaped tsp mustard – wholegrain or Dijon
2 tbsp freshly chopped herbs, such as mint, parsley, chives, or a mixture
1 bread slice
1 small onion
1 garlic clove
1 medium egg
250g/9 oz lean minced lamb
1 tsp mixed spice, cumin or curry powder
Freshly milled salt and black pepper
2 tsp olive oil

1. Stir the yogurt with the mustard and herbs and set aside.

2. Tear the bread into small pieces and put into a mixing bowl. Sprinkle it with 2 tbsp water.

3. Chop the onion very finely (or grate it coarsely). Finely chop or crush the garlic. Lightly beat the egg.

4. Add the lamb to the bread and sprinkle the spice or cumin or curry powder over. Season with salt and pepper. Add the onion, garlic and egg and mix well (with your hands or a fork).

5. Heat a shallow, non-stick frying pan and add the oil. Spoon a small amount of lamb into the hot pan and flatten it slightly. Repeat with the remaining lamb, cooking for 2–3 minutes on each side until golden brown and cooked through.

6. Heat your chosen wraps (see page 80). Serve hot with the yogurt dressing.

Hot Chilli Beef, Bean and Spinach Wraps

A perfect combination, hot spicy meat and beans are complemented by the cool soured cream and the flour tortillas. As you assemble the wraps, the heat from the beef wilts the spinach leaves – delicious!

Serves 4

2 red chillies (see page 8)
1 red onion
4 tomatoes
1 red pepper
1 garlic clove
200g can red kidney beans or chickpeas
Small spinach leaves
1 tsp oil
175g/6 oz lean minced beef
1 beef stock cube
Freshly milled salt and pepper
4 soft flour tortilla wraps
Soured cream

1. Halve the chillies, remove and discard the seeds and slice thinly. Thinly slice the onion and chop the tomatoes. Halve the pepper, remove and discard its seeds and stalk, and slice thinly. Crush the garlic clove and drain the red kidney beans or chickpeas. Wash the spinach leaves if necessary and shake dry.

2. Heat a saucepan, add the oil and minced beef. Cook over a medium heat for 5 minutes, breaking the mince into small pieces with a spoon.

3. Stir in the chillies, tomatoes, pepper, garlic, red kidney beans or chickpeas, stock cube and 150ml/¼ pint boiling water. Bring just to the boil, reduce the heat and cook for 10 minutes. Season to taste.

4. Heat the wraps (see page 80). Scatter some of the spinach leaves and red onion over each wrap, spoon the mince mixture down the centre and add a blob of soured cream.

5. Tightly roll the wrap over the filling and cut each in half. Serve immediately with extra soured cream.

10

SMART DINING FOR ONE & TWO

Dining alone or *à deux*? No reason to stint yourself or dumb down. Instead, go for a delicious meal that is also fun to prepare. Cooking for one or two opens up the way to some great dishes, which for a larger number of people would usually be too difficult or just too much effort to make. Food, for example, that needs plenty of room in the pan: whole fish, steaks, gammon and omelettes, all included in this section. Or try the recipe for homemade ravioli on page 90.

pasta triangles filled with crab and prawns

Large Pasta Triangles Filled with Crab and Prawns

An unusual use of fresh lasagne sheets – jumbo ravioli. You could replace the fishy ingredients with cooked and finely chopped smoked chicken or ham. Serve them with a crisp green salad.

Serves 2

1 lemon
1 medium egg
75g/2¾ oz cooked shelled prawns, thawed if frozen
100g/3½ oz cooked crabmeat
2 tsp sweet chilli sauce
Freshly milled black pepper
6 fresh lasagne sheets
150ml/¼ pint chicken stock
150ml/¼ pint fish stock
2 tbsp freshly chopped chives
2 tbsp dry white vermouth
25g/1 oz butter

1. Finely grate the rind from the lemon, halve and squeeze out the juice. Break the egg into a small bowl and beat lightly with a fork.
2. Finely chop the prawns, flake the crabmeat and mix together in a small bowl. Stir in the chilli sauce, a little seasoning and up to half the beaten egg, just enough to bind the mixture.
3. If the lasagne sheets are oblong, trim them to make squares. Keep the pasta covered with cling film or damp kitchen paper to prevent it from drying out.
4. To make the pasta triangles: take a pasta sheet and brush the edges with a little egg. Put a little of the prawn and crab filling in the centre, fold the pasta over the filling and press the edges gently to seal them. Repeat with the remaining pasta and filling.
5. Meanwhile pour the two stocks into a large, shallow pan. Add the lemon rind and lemon juice and bring to the boil. Reduce the heat a little (the pasta must not swirl around the pan too much otherwise it will split), carefully lower the pasta into the liquid and cook gently for 10–12 minutes. With a slotted spoon, lift the pasta into bowls and keep warm.
6. Quickly increase the heat, stir in the chives, vermouth and butter. Cook until slightly thickened, spoon over the pasta triangles and serve immediately.

Fish with Caper Drizzle Sauce

This is a striking dish that is a special treat. Choose a firm fish such as sea bass or trout (ask the fishmonger to clean it), and make sure it will fit your pan. Lovely served with new potatoes glazed with a little extra virgin olive oil.

Serves 1 or 2

1 lemon
Large bunch of dill
1 tbsp capers
1 whole fish, such as sea bass (see note above)
1 tbsp olive oil
25g/1 oz butter
4 tbsp dry vermouth or white wine
Freshly milled salt and pepper

1. Cut the lemon into six wedges. Chop the dill. Rinse, dry and chop the capers.

2. Tuck four lemon wedges and half the dill into the cavity of the fish.

3. Heat a non-stick frying pan and add the oil and butter. Add the fish and brown quickly on both sides.

4. Sprinkle over 3 tbsp vermouth or wine and the capers. Cover and cook gently for about 12–15 minutes or until the fish is just cooked through.

5. Carefully lift the fish out of the pan and keep warm.

6. Add the remaining vermouth or wine to the pan, bring just to the boil and bubble for a minute. Stir in the remaining dill and season if necessary.

7. Drizzle the juices over the fish and serve with the remaining lemon wedges for squeezing over.

Fish in a Crust with Tartare Sauce

Cornmeal gives a crisp golden crust. Make sure the fish pieces will fit in the pan side by side. If they are just too big, keep the first one warm while you cook the second. Good served with a salad of sliced tomatoes and sprigs of watercress. To make this dish for one, use the same quantities to coat the fish. You could halve the sauce but why not make the full amount and serve it as a dip, with freshly cooked vegetables, on steak or as a sandwich spread?

Serves 2

Tartare Sauce:
1 gherkin
2 tsp capers
Small handful of fresh parsley
150ml/¼ pint mayonnaise

1 small egg
50g/1¾ oz cornmeal (polenta)
25g/1 oz plain flour
2 tbsp freshly chopped parsley
Freshly milled salt and pepper
2 pieces of fish, such as skate wings, plaice fillets or salmon steaks
Oil for cooking
Lemon wedges, for serving

1. To make the tartare sauce, chop the gherkin, capers and parsley very finely and stir them into the mayonnaise. Cover and leave to stand.
2. Break the egg onto a large, wide, shallow dish and beat. On another wide dish, mix the cornmeal with the flour, chopped parsley and a little seasoning.
3. Take one piece of fish and dip it first in the egg, coating it well and shaking off any excess. Now dip the eggy fish in the cornmeal mixture, making sure it is well covered. Repeat with the second piece of fish.
4. Heat some oil in a large frying pan. When hot, add the fish and cook over a medium heat for about 5 minutes each side, or until just cooked through.
5. Drain on kitchen paper and serve immediately with lemon wedges and the tartare sauce.

Herb and Bacon Omelette

Smoked bacon adds its own distinctive flavour to the omelette. For a more substantial meal, serve it with a bowl of salad and some crusty bread.

Serves 1

2 lettuce leaves
1 smoked back bacon rasher
2 medium eggs
1 tsp freshly chopped parsley
1 tsp freshly chopped chives
Freshly milled black pepper
Small piece of butter
2 tsp freshly grated Parmesan cheese

1.　Finely shred the lettuce leaves. With scissors, trim the rind from the bacon rasher and cut the bacon into small pieces. Break the eggs into a bowl and add 1 tbsp cold water, the parsley and the chives. Season with pepper.

2.　Heat a small frying pan, add the bacon pieces and, without adding any fat, cook quickly for a few minutes, stirring occasionally, until golden brown. Lift out of the pan.

3.　Put the butter and shredded lettuce in the hot pan and cook gently until the butter has melted and the lettuce has wilted.

4.　Return the bacon to the pan, pour the egg mixture over and cook gently, drawing the set mixture away from the sides of the pan to the centre (the liquid egg will run and fill the gaps – don't stir too much otherwise you will have scrambled eggs).

5.　When the omelette is soft on the top and golden brown underneath, sprinkle the cheese over and brown quickly under a hot grill.

6.　Serve immediately.

Pasta and Bacon in a Creamy Egg Sauce

Our version of "spaghetti carbonara". You could cook this using just one large pan – cook the pasta first, then leave in a colander to drain while you use the same pan to cook the bacon. In step 5, remember to take the pan off the heat or the egg may scramble instead of simply thickening gently into a smooth sauce.

Serves 2

50g/1¾ oz Parmesan cheese, preferably in one piece
5 tbsp double cream
1 egg yolk
1 tbsp freshly chopped parsley or chives
4 lean bacon rashers
150g/5½ oz spaghetti
1 tbsp olive oil
4 tbsp dry white vermouth or wine
Freshly milled pepper

1. Finely grate the Parmesan cheese. Stir together the cream, egg yolk and parsley or chives. With scissors, trim the rind from the bacon rashers and cut the bacon into small strips.

2. Cook the spaghetti following the packet instructions.

3. Meanwhile, heat a second large pan, add the oil and bacon and cook over a medium heat, stirring occasionally until the bacon begins to turn golden brown. Add the vermouth or wine and bubble very gently for 1–2 minutes.

4. When the pasta is cooked, drain and add it to the bacon mixture. Toss gently over a low heat and season with pepper.

5. Remove the pan from the heat and add the cream mixture and half the cheese. Toss everything together gently (the sauce will thicken as it meets the heat of the pan and the spaghetti).

6. Tip into warmed bowls and sprinkle the remaining Parmesan cheese over the top.

Frikadeller with an Orange Glaze

These mini burgers can be rustled up in minutes. Though the nutmeg is optional, it makes all the difference to the flavour. Redcurrant or cranberry jelly makes a good alternative to marmalade in the sauce. To make this dish for one, halve the ingredients, replacing the onion with a shallot.

Serves 2

1 small onion
1 small egg
250g/9 oz lean minced pork
25g/1 oz plain flour
Pinch of grated nutmeg (optional)
Freshly milled salt and black pepper
1 tbsp oil
2 tbsp orange marmalade, preferably thin cut
1–2 tbsp thick yogurt or soured cream

1. Finely chop or grate the onion. Break the egg into a mixing bowl and add the pork, onion, flour, nutmeg (if using) and a little seasoning. With your hands or a spoon, mix well. Roughly divide the mixture into four.

2. Heat the oil in a wide, non-stick frying pan. When hot, spoon the pork mixture into the pan, one portion at a time and flattening them slightly, making sure they do not touch.

3. Cook over a medium heat for 5–8 minutes on each side until golden brown and cooked through. Lift out and keep warm.

4. Add the marmalade to the hot pan juices and heat gently until melted, adding a splash of water if necessary.

5. Return the burgers to the pan and turn them in the hot orange sauce until coated.

6. Serve drizzled with yogurt or soured cream.

Sticky Gammon with Carrot and Parsnip Mash

A perfect dish for one as gammon steaks take up a lot of space during cooking. If you want to cook for two, use a really large frying pan.

Serves 1

1 large parsnip
2 medium carrots
1 small orange
1 shallot
1 gammon steak
1 tsp oil
2 tsp brown sugar
A few raisins
½ tsp vegetable bouillon
Freshly milled black pepper
2 tbsp milk
1 tsp butter

1. Peel and chop the parsnip and carrots. Finely grate the rind from the orange, halve and squeeze out the juice. Slice the shallot. Snip the rind on the gammon steak in two or three places (to prevent it from curling up during cooking).

2. Put the parsnip and carrots into a pan of boiling water and cook for 8–10 minutes until soft.

3. Heat the oil in a frying pan, add the gammon steak and cook quickly on both sides until golden brown. Lift from the pan.

4. Add the shallot to the pan and cook over a medium heat for a few minutes, stirring once or twice, until softened. Stir in the orange rind and orange juice, brown sugar, raisins, bouillon and 3–4 tbsp water. Stirring, bring just to the boil, reduce the heat, return the gammon steak to the pan and cook for 5 minutes, turning once, or until cooked through. Add a little more water if it becomes too dry and season if necessary.

5. Meanwhile drain the vegetables, add the milk and butter and crush or mash with a fork or potato masher.

6. Lift the gammon steak onto a warmed plate and pour the sauce over. Add the mash and serve immediately.

Beef Steaks with Mango Salsa

This meal for two is ideal for a special occasion – it's simple to make, yet impressive. When cooking for one, just halve the ingredients. The salsa is delicious made with mango, but peaches, nectarines or plums would be equally good. Serve with green salad and French bread.

Serves 2

1 small red onion
4 tomatoes
½ red pepper
1 garlic clove
1 small ripe mango
Small bunch of coriander
8 mixed peppercorns (green, pink and black)
2 rump steaks
Oil
Freshly milled salt and pepper
Soured cream, to serve

1. Chop the onion and tomatoes quite finely. Remove and discard the seeds and stalk from the pepper and chop finely. Crush the garlic clove. Peel the mango, cut the flesh away from the stone and dice. Chop the coriander. Put everything in a bowl, mix and leave to stand for 20 minutes if possible, for the flavours of the salsa to mingle and develop.

2. Put the peppercorns on a chopping board and crush with a rolling pin.

3. Pat the steaks dry with kitchen paper and press the crushed peppercorns on both sides.

4. Heat a griddle pan or frying pan, add a little oil and when hot cook the steaks until browned on both sides – a total of 3–4 minutes for rare, 5–6 minutes for medium-rare, 6–8 minutes for medium and 10 minutes for well done. Season if necessary.

5. Serve the steaks with the mango salsa and a spoonful of soured cream.

11

FAMILY EATS

Nice 'n' easy does it. Here are some really easy, totally unchallenging recipes. These meals are firm family favourites (they certainly are in our families!). Ideal for weekdays, they are just as good at the weekend, and they will appeal to young and old alike.

Whether you want eggs or sausages, fish or chicken, lamb or pork, it's all here – and there's even a tailor-made burger on page 106. Basic dishes they may be, but each one has a novel twist of its own. They all serve four.

s a u s a g e s   w i t h   a t t i t u d e

Spanish Potato Tortilla

Try our version of this thick potato omelette from Spain. If you use a flameproof pan, instead of turning the omelette over, you could brown the top under a hot grill in step 8. Serve with tomato wedges and some crusty bread.

Serves 4

4 medium potatoes
2 Spanish onions
2 large peppers, red and green
2 garlic cloves
6 large eggs
150ml/¼ pint single cream or milk
3 tbsp freshly chopped parsley
Freshly milled salt and pepper
2 tbsp olive oil, plus extra if required
Small piece of butter

1. Peel and thinly slice the potatoes. Chop the onions. Halve the red and green peppers, remove and discard the seeds and stalks, and slice thinly. Crush the garlic cloves.

2. Break the eggs into a bowl, stir in the cream or milk and the parsley and season to taste.

3. Arrange the potatoes over the base of a large, non-stick frying pan, cover with boiling water and cook for 5 minutes. Drain well and put to one side.

4. Clean the pan and reheat it. Put half the oil and butter into the hot pan, then add the chopped onions and cook over a medium heat for 5 minutes, stirring once or twice.

5. Stir in the red and green pepper slices and crushed garlic. Cook a further 3–4 minutes.

6. Reduce the heat, stir in the potato slices (it doesn't matter if some break) and pour the egg mixture over. Cook gently until the egg mixture has set.

7. Carefully invert the tortilla onto a large, flat plate.

8. Add the remaining oil and butter to the pan and carefully slide the tortilla back into the pan, browned side up. Cook gently until the second side has browned.

9. Serve, cut into wedges.

Hake on Tomato and Olive Sauce

You could use any white fish fillets or steaks in this recipe. It's good served with crusty bread, thick slices of hot toast or, our favourite, garlic bread.

Serves 4

2 leeks
1 garlic clove
1 tbsp olive oil
400g can chopped tomatoes
1 tsp sugar
¼ tsp chilli paste or a pinch of chilli powder (optional)
4 thick skinless fillets of hake, each weighing about
   175g/6 oz
Freshly milled salt and pepper
50g/1¾ oz pitted black olives
Chopped fresh herbs, such as parsley, chives or basil

1. Thinly slice the leeks and crush or finely chop the garlic.

2. Heat a large frying pan and add the oil, leeks and garlic. Cook gently for at least 5 minutes, stirring occasionally, until the leeks are soft but not browned.

3. Stir in the tomatoes, sugar and chilli (if using). Gently bring the mixture to the boil, stir and lower the heat.

4. Lay the fish on the tomato sauce, sprinkle with a little salt and pepper and scatter the olives over.

5. Cover and cook gently for about 10 minutes or until the fish is just cooked through.

6. Scatter with fresh herbs and serve.

Sausages with Attitude

A mixture of butchers' sausages, Spanish chorizo and smoked sausage gives a wonderful rich flavour to this dish. Mashed or sautéed potatoes go well with it.

Serves 4

1 large red onion
3 spicy pork sausages
125g/4½ oz chorizo sausage
125g/4½ oz smoked sausage
Small piece of fresh root ginger
8 button mushrooms
1 cooking apple, such as a Bramley
4 sage leaves
2 tbsp freshly chopped parsley
1 tbsp wholegrain mustard
300ml/½ pint vegetable stock
1 tsp cornflour
Freshly milled salt and pepper

1. Thinly slice the onion. Cut the pork sausages in half crossways, and thickly slice the chorizo and smoked sausage. Grate the ginger. Clean, trim and halve the mushrooms. Quarter the apple, remove and discard the core, and chop.

2. Heat a large, shallow, non-stick frying pan and (without adding fat) cook all the sausage pieces quickly for a few minutes until the juices begin to flow. Add the onion and cook for 5 minutes or until the sausage pieces are browned and almost cooked.

3. Stir in the chopped apple and halved mushrooms. Cook for 1 minute then add the grated ginger, sage, parsley, mustard and stock. Bring just to the boil, reduce the heat and cook gently until the apple has softened.

4. Put the cornflour in a small cup, add a little water and mix to a smooth paste.

5. Stir the cornflour paste into the pan, bring just to the boil and bubble for 1 minute. Season if necessary and serve.

Cumberland Sausages with Tomato and Vegetable Sauce

Choose Cumberland or your favourite meaty sausages for this recipe. Serve it with a mash made with potatoes, root vegetables (parsnips, carrots, swede) or instant polenta.

Serves 4

1 medium onion
3 medium carrots
2 garlic cloves
1 lemon
1 tbsp oil
8 large sausages
400g can chopped tomatoes
2 tbsp tomato purée
2 tsp sugar
250ml/9 fl oz vegetable stock
Freshly milled salt and black pepper
3 tbsp freshly chopped parsley

1. Finely chop the onion, thinly slice the carrots and crush the garlic. Finely grate the rind from the lemon.

2. Heat the oil in a large frying pan, add the sausages and brown quickly on all sides. Lift out.

3. To the pan, add the onion, carrots and garlic. Cook over a medium heat for about 5 minutes, stirring occasionally, until they begin to soften and turn golden brown. Stir in the tomatoes, tomato purée, sugar, stock and seasoning.

4. Bring just to the boil and add the sausages, pushing them into the sauce. Cook over a medium heat for about 10 minutes or until the sausages are cooked through.

5. Mix together the lemon rind and parsley. Just before serving, sprinkle the mixture over the contents of the pan.

Chicken with Green Sauce

Instead of using mini chicken fillets, you could of course cut some chicken breast meat into strips. Or why not use turkey or pork? Serve with baby potatoes, rice or pasta.

Serves 4

1 green pepper
Small bunch of fresh parsley
Few sprigs of fresh thyme
1 onion
¼ small savoy cabbage
1 tbsp plain flour
Freshly milled salt and pepper
450g/1 lb mini chicken fillets
1 tbsp oil
300ml/½ pint chicken stock
150ml/¼ pint unsweetened orange juice
200ml carton low-fat crème fraîche
175g/6 oz fresh podded peas

1. Halve the pepper, remove and discard the seeds and stalk, and slice thinly. Chop the parsley and strip the leaves from the thyme. Chop the onion and thinly slice the cabbage.

2. Tip the flour onto a plate and season with salt and pepper. Turn the chicken fillets in the flour until lightly dusted.

3. Heat a large frying pan and add the oil and chicken pieces. Cook gently for at least 5 minutes on both sides until browned. Add the stock and orange juice, and stir in the green pepper and half the thyme leaves. Cover and cook gently for 15 minutes or until cooked through.

4. Stir in the crème fraîche, parsley and remaining thyme leaves and cook gently, uncovered, for 5 minutes. Season to taste.

5. Meanwhile, in another pan cook the peas and cabbage in a little boiling water for a few minutes until just cooked then drain.

6. Stir the drained peas and cabbage into the main pan and serve.

Lamb with Leeks, Rosemary and Honey

The number of lamb chops used will depend on their size and your appetite. When time allows (or with a little forward planning), we like to marinate the lamb in the oil-and-rosemary mixture for a couple of hours or even overnight – just put the bag on a plate in the fridge, turning it once or twice if you get the chance. The lamb is good served alongside a creamy mash made with potato, squash or celeriac, or a mixture.

Serves 4

3 tbsp olive oil
2 tbsp wine vinegar or lemon juice
1 tbsp freshly chopped rosemary leaves, plus 1 sprig
Freshly milled salt and black pepper
4–8 lamb chops, such as loin
400g/14 oz leeks
1 garlic clove
5 tbsp double cream
2 tsp clear honey

1. Put half the oil into a large food (freezer) bag, add the wine vinegar or lemon juice, chopped rosemary and a little seasoning. Add the lamb and turn in the mixture, coating it well (see note above).

2. Thinly slice the leeks and finely chop or crush the garlic.

3. Heat a large frying pan (preferably non-stick) and add the remaining oil. Add the lamb chops in a single layer and cook quickly for about 6 minutes on each side, or until browned and cooked to your liking. Lift out and keep warm.

4. Drain off any excess fat from the pan, then stir in the leeks, garlic and rosemary sprig (stir in any sediments from the bottom of the pan). Cook over a medium heat for about 5 minutes, stirring occasionally, until the leeks are soft. Remove from the heat.

5. Stir the cream and honey into the leeks and return the lamb chops to the pan. Cook gently until bubbling and add a little seasoning if necessary. Remove the rosemary sprig before serving.

Chinese Spiced Pepper Pork

Five-spice powder is a mixture of five ground spices – cloves, cinnamon, fennel seeds, star anise and Szechwan peppercorns – and is easily obtainable in supermarkets. The recipe works equally well with chicken. Serve it with cooked rice or noodles.

Serves 4

3 spring onions
2 peppers, red and/or orange
2 garlic cloves
2 courgettes
2 red chillies (see page 8)
450g/1 lb lean pork
3 tbsp cornflour
2 tsp five-spice powder
Freshly milled pepper
2 tbsp vegetable oil, plus extra if required
1 tbsp soy sauce
1 pork or chicken stock cube
1 tsp cider vinegar
1 tsp clear honey
3 tbsp freshly chopped parsley

1. Chop the spring onions. Halve the red and orange peppers, remove and discard the seeds and stalks, and slice thinly. Crush the garlic cloves and roughly chop the courgettes. Cut the chillies in half, remove and discard the seeds, and slice thinly. Trim any fat from the pork and cut into strips.
2. Mix the cornflour, five-spice powder and seasoning in a food (freezer) bag. Add the pork strips and shake until thoroughly coated.
3. Heat a wok or large pan and pour in the oil. When hot stir-fry the pork a few pieces at a time until golden and cooked through. Remove with a slotted spoon and cook the remaining meat.
4. Add a little more oil to the wok if necessary, heat and tip in the garlic, chillies, sliced spring onions, peppers and courgettes. Stir-fry for 2–3 minutes.
5. Stir in the soy sauce, stock cube, 150ml/¼ pint water, cider vinegar and honey. Bring just to the boil and stir in the pork strips and chopped parsley. Cook quickly for 2–3 minutes and serve.

Burgers

Follow the basic method, customising your burgers according to your mood of the moment. There are plenty of ideas here. If you need even more inspiration, think of adding one or more of the following to the burger mix: finely chopped red or green pepper, a few chopped walnuts or unsalted peanuts, grated root ginger, tomato purée, chopped fresh chilli or curry paste.

Makes 4

500g/1 lb 2 oz lean minced meat
1 medium onion
Freshly milled salt and black pepper
Vegetable oil for cooking

For beef, add:
1 crushed garlic clove
1–2 tbsp ready-made mustard or horseradish sauce
Small handful of freshly chopped parsley

For pork, add:
1–2 tbsp ready-made apple sauce
2 tsp chopped fresh sage
Small handful of chopped chives

For lamb, add:
1 crushed garlic clove
1–2 tbsp redcurrant jelly or cranberry sauce
Small handful of freshly chopped mint

For chicken or turkey, add:
Finely grated rind of 1 small lemon
1 tbsp thyme leaves
Small handful of freshly chopped parsley

For venison, add:
Finely grated rind of 1 small orange
1 tsp ground allspice or cardamom
Small handful of freshly chopped parsley

1. Put the minced meat into a mixing bowl. Finely chop the onion and add to the meat. Season with salt and pepper and add your chosen flavourings from the lists opposite. With a fork, mix together well.

2. With wetted hands, divide and shape the mixture into four burgers.

3. Heat a large frying pan, preferably non-stick, and add a little oil. Arrange the burgers in the pan in a single layer and cook on a medium heat for 4–6 minutes each side or until done. Beef, lamb and venison can be served pink in the middle. Pork, chicken and turkey must be cooked right through.

To assemble:

Split some burger buns or pitta breads and spread on some wholegrain mustard or your favourite relish. Add some crisp salad leaves and tomato slices. Put the burger on the salad bits, and top with sliced gherkins or pickles, and maybe even a slice of cheese. Add a squirt of mayonnaise or tomato ketchup (or both!) and perch the bun lid on top.

12

FEASTS FOR FRIENDS

To give some added lustre to your convivial entertaining, here are some of the recipes we like to think of as special. Deceptively simple to make, they are ideally suited to sharing with friends. The ingredients should be just a bit classy – maybe a little more expensive than usual, with some alcohol splashed in. The results will be memorable.

Dishes like fondue and mussels are perfect whenever you have the luxury of being able to linger, long and late, over your evening meal, chatting with your friends and putting the world to rights.

Have a look at 'Take One Big Shallow Pan' too, on pages 73–79. Most of these recipes are great for serving to friends too.

lamb medallions

Two Cheese Fondue

A perennial favourite, particularly when the weather is icy. It's best to use an earthenware or flameproof dish – metal makes the cheese mixture too hot. We like the nutty-sweet flavour of this Emmenthal and Gruyère mix but you could use a combination of your favourite types of hard cheese instead. Kirsch is the traditional cherry brandy here – use a miniature bottle.

Serves 4–6

Bread
**A selection of button mushrooms, radishes, courgettes,
  carrots, cherry tomatoes, spring onions**
1 garlic clove
225g/8 oz Emmenthal cheese
225g/8 oz Gruyère cheese
1 tsp cornflour
Pinch of mustard powder
3 tbsp cherry brandy
300ml/½ pint dry white wine
Pinch of ground nutmeg
Freshly milled salt and white pepper

1. Prepare the bread and vegetables to serve with the fondue. Tear the bread into chunky pieces. Clean and trim the vegetables and cut into chunks, sticks or thick slices.

2. Cut the garlic clove in half. Grate the cheeses. In a small bowl mix together the cornflour, mustard powder and cherry brandy.

3. Rub the inside of an earthenware fondue or flameproof dish with the cut surface of the garlic. Pour in the wine and heat very slowly. With a wooden spoon, stir the grated cheeses into the wine and heat slowly until melted (it helps to stir the mixture occasionally).

4. Stir the blended cornflour into the melted cheese mixture and cook gently for 2–3 minutes until thick and creamy (but not boiling), stirring occasionally.

5. Season to taste with the nutmeg, salt and pepper. Serve the fondue at the table, keeping the dish warm over a spirit warmer or a plate warmer.

6. Serve with the bread and vegetables to spear and dunk into the hot creamy fondue.

Fish and Prawn Coconut Curry

Suitable accompaniments might include poppadoms or naan bread, mango chutney and a simple salad made with thin slices of tomato and red onion. Or you could put some rice on the hob to cook at the same time as the fish – once the rice has cooked, try stirring in a little butter, lemon juice and finely grated lemon rind.

Serves 4–6

1 large onion
1 small lemon
100g/3½ oz creamed coconut (available in a block)
**About 500g/1 lb 2 oz skinless fish, such as cod, haddock
  or salmon**
**About 500g/1 lb 2 oz cooked shelled prawns, thawed if
  frozen**
2 tbsp oil
1 tbsp mild or medium curry powder
1 tbsp tomato purée
500ml/18 fl oz vegetable or fish stock
Fresh coriander leaves

1. Thinly slice the onion. Finely grate the rind from the lemon, cut in half and squeeze out the juice. Chop the coconut into small pieces. Cut the fish into large chunks. Rinse, drain and dry the prawns.

2. Heat the oil in a large, deep frying pan or wok. Add the onion and cook for about 5 minutes, stirring occasionally, until softened and only just beginning to turn golden brown.

3. Stir the curry powder into the onion and cook for 1 minute, stirring.

4. Add the tomato purée, coconut, lemon rind and juice, and stock. Heat, stirring, until bubbling and well mixed. (The sauce can be prepared to this stage then covered and left to stand. Just before you want to serve up, reheat the sauce and continue with step 5.)

5. Stir in the fish and prawns and cook very gently for about 5 minutes until just cooked through.

6. Serve immediately with coriander leaves scattered over the top.

Mussels in Cider and Mint Sauce

Serve in large, shallow bowls with plenty of fresh crusty bread to mop up the sauce. For a classic Moules Marinière, replace the cider with dry white wine and the mint with parsley.

Serves 4 as a starter or 2 as a main dish

1.8kg/4 lb mussels in their shells
1 bunch of spring onions
1 garlic clove
2 tbsp olive oil
150ml/¼ pint dry cider
Freshly milled black pepper
2–3 tbsp crème fraîche
2–3 tbsp chopped fresh mint

1. Scrub the mussels, discarding any with broken shells or that do not close when given a sharp knock. Pull off the beards (the black hairy tufts hanging out of the shell).

2. Thickly slice the spring onions. Finely chop or crush the garlic.

3. Put the oil and garlic into a very large pan and heat through without allowing the garlic to brown.

4. Add the cider, spring onions and some black pepper, then tip in the mussels. Cover with a lid and cook quickly for 4–5 minutes, shaking the pan occasionally, until the mussels have just opened (discard any that haven't).

5. Remove the lid and stir in the crème fraîche and mint.

6. Bubble gently for a minute or two then serve.

Oyster Mushrooms and Turkey in a Creamy Thyme Sauce

An elegant dish to serve to friends. Remember not to let the sauce boil after the soured cream has been added in step 6 or it may curdle. Serve it with fragrant rice, noodles or French bread.

Serves 4

450g/1 lb skinless, boneless turkey breast, skin removed
1 large onion
175g/6 oz oyster mushrooms
6 sprigs of fresh thyme
2 tbsp plain flour
½ tsp ground paprika pepper
Freshly milled salt and black pepper
2 tbsp olive oil
150ml/¼ pint vegetable stock
300ml/½ pint soured cream

1. Cut the turkey breast into thin strips and thinly slice the onion. Clean and trim the mushrooms and tear into pieces. Strip the thyme leaves from the stalks.

2. Tip the flour into a bowl or a food (freezer) bag and season with paprika, salt and pepper. Add the turkey strips and turn in the seasoned flour until coated.

3. Heat half the oil in a non-stick pan, stir in the chopped onion and cook for 5 minutes until golden. Add the mushrooms and cook for a further 2–3 minutes. Using a slotted spoon, lift the vegetables onto a plate.

4. Heat the remaining oil in the pan, add the turkey pieces and cook over a medium heat for about 10 minutes, stirring occasionally, until golden brown and cooked through.

5. Return the vegetables to the pan, pour the stock over and add the thyme leaves. Bring just to the boil and cook gently for 5 minutes, stirring once or twice.

6. Add the soured cream, stirring once or twice until mixed. Heat through for 2–3 minutes until piping hot and serve immediately.

Lamb Medallions with Wild Mushrooms and Vermouth

Don't be tempted to cut the mushrooms too small – they look more attractive if left whole or torn into large pieces. New potatoes or noodles go well with it.

Serves 4

225g/8 oz mixed mushrooms, such as chestnut, shiitake, oyster
1 onion
Small bunch of fresh parsley
450g/1 lb lamb neck fillet
Freshly milled black pepper
1 tbsp oil
300ml/½ pint lamb or vegetable stock
150ml/¼ pint dry white vermouth
4 thyme sprigs
1 bay leaf
150ml/¼ pint crème fraîche
1 tbsp brandy

1. Clean and trim the mushrooms, tearing them in half if large. Finely chop the onion and chop the parsley.
2. Cut the lamb into eight thick slices or medallions. Pat dry with kitchen paper, slightly flatten each medallion with the palm of your hand. Season with pepper.
3. Heat half the oil in a wide pan, stir in the chopped onion and cook for 5 minutes, stirring once or twice, until golden.
4. Add the mushrooms and cook for 2–3 minutes. With a slotted spoon lift out the vegetables.
5. Heat the remaining oil, add the lamb and cook quickly for 3–4 minutes on both sides until golden. Lift out of the pan and keep warm.
6. Pour the stock and vermouth into the pan, bring to the boil, mixing in any sediment stuck to the pan, and cook for about 2 minutes until bubbling.
7. Return the vegetables and lamb to the pan, stir in the thyme sprigs, bay leaf and chopped parsley. Bring just to the boil, reduce the heat and cook gently for 5 minutes. Stir in the crème fraîche and brandy, heat until piping hot and serve immediately.

Venison Steaks with Cranberries and Chestnuts in a Red Wine Sauce

No need to shell chestnuts. Use the ready peeled and cooked versions that you can buy all year round in cans or vacuum packs, or from the freezer. Fragrant rice makes a lovely accompaniment here.

Serves 4

1 large red onion
1 garlic clove
85g/3 oz shelled cooked chestnuts (see note above)
Freshly milled black pepper
4 venison steaks
1 tbsp olive oil
100g/3½ oz fresh cranberries, thawed if frozen
150ml/¼ pint dry red wine
300ml/½ pint vegetable stock

1. Chop the onion finely and crush the garlic. Halve the chestnuts. Pat the steaks dry with kitchen paper and season.

2. Heat a wide, shallow pan, add the oil and onion and cook over a medium heat for a few minutes until the onion is soft and lightly browned. With a slotted spoon lift the onion onto a plate and keep warm.

3. Put the steaks into the hot pan and quickly brown both the sides and the edges. Reduce the heat to medium and cook for 10 minutes, turning occasionally. The steaks will be rare – cook a little longer if you prefer medium or well cooked. Lift out of the pan and keep warm.

4. Return the onion to the hot pan, increase the heat, stir in the crushed garlic and cranberries and cook for a minute in the pan juices. Pour in the red wine and stock and stir in the chestnuts. Bring just to the boil, reduce the heat and cook gently for about 5 minutes or until the cranberries have softened and the sauce has reduced slightly.

5. Cut each steak into three or four slices and arrange on warmed plates. Spoon the sauce mixture over and serve.

13

PUDS IN A FLASH

Can we tempt you to a pudding? Are you a member of the sweet tooth brigade? We are, like most people we know. Puddings are an indulgence, and most of the time you probably just grab a yogurt or an ice cream. So here are the quickest, easiest desserts you will ever make.

To round off a dinner, when pudding is a must, or at any time of the day whenever the need is great, this choice of desserts is at your command. Some are light and fruity, some creamy, some sticky and gooey or intensely chocolatey. All of them have a touch of glamour. So don't hold back!

boozy pan-fried apples

Redcurrant and Red Plum Fool

What is a fool? It's sheer luxury! After scraping out the vanilla seeds, don't discard the empty pod – put it into a container of sugar and it will impart its delicate flavour. You will need some crisp biscuits to serve with it.

Serves 6

280g/10 oz red plums
225g/8 oz redcurrants
1 vanilla pod
3 tbsp orange juice
3 tbsp clear honey
300ml/½ pint ready-made custard
300ml/½ pint natural yogurt
300ml/½ pint fromage frais

1. Halve the plums, remove the stones and cut each half into four pieces.

2. Strip the redcurrants from the stalks, reserving a few for decoration.

3. Slit open the vanilla pod and scrape out the seeds.

4. Heat a small pan and add the plums, redcurrants, vanilla seeds, orange juice and honey. Bring just to the boil, reduce the heat and cook gently until the fruits have just begun to collapse.

5. Remove from the heat and stir in the custard.

6. To serve this dessert warm, carefully fold in the yogurt and fromage frais, spoon into serving dishes, decorate with the reserved redcurrants and serve immediately. If you prefer a cold dessert, chill the fruit-custard mixture, then fold in the yogurt and fromage frais, spoon into glasses and chill until required. Before serving, decorate with the reserved redcurrants.

Whisky Oatmeal Cream with Apricots

A taste of Scotland – oatmeal, whisky and heather honey. Carry on the theme by serving it with shortbread biscuits.

Serves 4–6

25g/1 oz medium oatmeal
175g/6 oz fresh ripe apricots
300ml/½ pint double cream
300ml/½ pint crème fraîche
3 tbsp clear honey, such as heather
6 tbsp whisky
2 tbsp fresh unsweetened orange juice

1. Heat a pan until hot, tip in the oatmeal and shake over the heat until very lightly toasted. (Take care it doesn't burn, the oatmeal will continue browning even after it's removed from the heat.) Tip onto a plate, spread out and leave to cool.

2. Meanwhile halve the apricots, remove the stones and cut each half into four pieces. Reserve a few for decoration. Lightly whip the cream until thickened but not stiff.

3. Spoon the crème fraîche into a bowl and mix in the honey, whisky and orange juice.

4. Carefully stir in the whipped cream and three quarters of the toasted oatmeal, taking care not to over mix.

5. Spoon the apricots into glasses or dishes and top with the creamy mixture. Sprinkle the remaining oatmeal over and decorate with the reserved apricot pieces.

Zabaglione with Mango and Sharon Fruit

One of Italy's most famous desserts, the warm foam sits on top of fresh fruit and crisp biscuit crumbs. Madeira makes a good alternative if you have no Marsala. It's best to use a hand-held electric mixer in step 3, though you could of course use a balloon whisk and lots of energy.

Serves 6

1 ripe mango
1 Sharon fruit
6 amaretti biscuits
2 tbsp almond liqueur
6 medium egg yolks
60g/2¼ oz caster sugar
6 tbsp sweet Marsala wine

1. Peel the mango, cut the flesh away from the stone and chop roughly. Remove the stalk from the Sharon fruit and cut into small pieces.

2. Roughly crush the biscuits and divide them between six glasses or dishes. Spoon the fruits on top. Sprinkle over a little almond liqueur, which will soak into the fruits and biscuits.

3. Bring a pan of water to the boil and place a bowl on top, making sure the base of the bowl doesn't touch the water. Put the egg yolks, sugar and Marsala into the bowl and, with a hand-held electric mixer, whisk until it turns into a thick, creamy foam.

4. Pour over the soaked fruits and serve immediately.

Boozy Pan-Fried Apples

You can't get much faster than this! Serve the apples just as they are, with thick yogurt, cream or crème fraîche. They also make a delicious filling for pancakes or a topping for toasted fruit bread or brioche.

Serves 2

2 eating apples
25g/1 oz butter
½ tsp ground cardamom or cinnamon
2 tbsp soft brown sugar
1 tsp lemon or lime juice
1 tbsp brandy or rum

1. Quarter the apples, remove and discard the cores, and cut into thick wedges.

2. Melt the butter in a small-to-medium, non-stick frying pan and stir in the cardamom or cinnamon. When the butter begins to sizzle, add the apples and cook quickly, turning them once, until golden brown on both sides.

3. Add the sugar, lemon or lime juice and brandy or rum, stirring until the sugar has dissolved.

4. Serve immediately.

Bananas in Butterscotch Sauce

A favourite fast pud that's good served with a scoop of vanilla or chocolate ice cream. Golden syrup is easy to measure if you warm the metal spoon first – just dunk it into hot water and quickly wipe dry before dipping it into the syrup.

Serves 2–3

25g/1 oz butter
25g/1 oz soft brown sugar
4 level tbsp golden syrup
1 tsp lemon juice
4 tbsp double cream
2 bananas
Chopped pecan nuts, to serve

1. Put the butter, sugar and syrup into a medium pan and heat very gently, stirring occasionally, until the butter has melted. Mix well, and then stir in the lemon juice and cream. Heat until bubbling.

2. Meanwhile, peel and cut the bananas into thick slices on the diagonal. Tip the bananas into the hot sauce and heat until the sauce just bubbles.

3. Stir and serve immediately, topped with a few chopped pecan nuts.

Glazed Pineapple Brioche with Coconut Cream

If you have one, cook the brioche and pineapple on a ridged griddle pan for those attractive barbecue stripes. Use fresh ripe or drained canned pineapple. No coconut liqueur in your booze cupboard? Use rum or brandy, or nothing at all.

Serves 2

1–2 tbsp coconut liqueur
150ml carton thick double cream
1 tbsp icing sugar
¼ tsp ground mixed spice
4 thick pineapple slices (see note above)
2 thick slices of brioche

1. Stir the coconut liqueur into the cream and leave on one side.

2. Combine the icing sugar and mixed spice and sprinkle over the pineapple.

3. Heat a griddle pan or non-stick frying pan. Add the brioche and cook over a medium heat until golden brown on both sides. Remove and keep warm.

4. Add the pineapple to the hot pan and cook quickly until sizzling and golden brown on both sides.

5. Lay the pineapple on the warm brioche and top with a generous spoonful of coconut cream.

Lime and Elderflower Curd Cheese Pancakes with Blueberries

Buy fresh blueberries when available, otherwise use frozen – thaw them first. In place of pancakes, you could toast some thick slices of brioche or fruit bread and top with the creamy elderflower mixture and blueberries.

Serves 4

175g/6 oz fresh blueberries
1 lime
250g carton curd cheese
3 tbsp elderflower syrup
150ml/¼ pint single cream
Milk, if needed
8 small ready-made traditional pancakes
Icing sugar, to dust

1. Clean the blueberries, removing any stalks or leaves.

2. With a potato peeler, thinly peel the lime (trying not to remove the white pith) and cut into very thin shreds. Cut the peeled lime in half and squeeze out the juice.

3. Spoon the curd cheese into a bowl and stir in the elderflower syrup, lime juice and half the lime shreds until just mixed. Slowly stir in the single cream, adding a little milk if the mixture is very stiff.

4. Spread some of the creamy lime filling over each pancake and roll up or fold over.

5. Put two pancakes on each serving plate, add some blueberries, dust with icing sugar and scatter the remaining shreds of lime over.

Chocolate Dip with Fruit and Nuts

Messy but sheer indulgence! Dip the goodies into the chocolate using cocktail sticks, forks or fingers.

It's easy to double, triple or quadruple the quantities to serve as many guests as you like.

Serves 2

A selection of fresh fruit, such as banana, ripe pear, peach, nectarine, strawberries
A selection of dried fruit, such as apricots and dates
A selection of whole nuts, such as brazils and almonds
100g/3½ oz plain chocolate
2 tbsp golden syrup
2 tsp lemon juice

1. Prepare the fruit, cutting it into large chunks, and arrange on a platter with the dried fruit and nuts.

2. Break the chocolate into a small pan and add the golden syrup, lemon juice and 1 tbsp water. Heat gently, stirring occasionally, until the chocolate has melted and the mixture is smooth and glossy. Pour into a warmed serving bowl.

3. Serve with the fruit and nuts for dipping.

INDEX

By the same authors

FRESH & FAST:
MEALS FROM THE OVEN

Prepare easy and delicious, nutritious, oven-cooked meals in a matter of minutes. Then sit back and relax, knowing that your dish is in the oven, until you're ready to eat.

Easily purchased fresh produce and a few store-cupboard ingredients are all you need, whether you're cooking for yourself, your family or friends.

Taste the difference! Widen your choice of fresh ingredients with these 100 recipes which will deliver bags of flavour, enjoyment and pleasure to your table.

Whichever meal it is, you'll find Annette Yates and Norma Miller have it covered, along with serving suggestions and plenty of hints and tips that make it all come together.

Uniform with this book